A RECIPE FOR LI

A RECIPE FOR LIFE

Elizabeth Anne Brown

2007

First published in 2007 by
Skoes Press

© Elizabeth Anne Brown

Designed and typeset by
CROFT PUBLICATIONS
The Croft, 8 St James Meadow, Borougbridge, YO51 9NW

Printed and bound by
SMITH SETTLE
Gateway Drive, Yeadon, West Yorkshire, LS19 7XY

CONTENTS

FOREWORD		vi
ACKNOWLEDGEMENTS		vii
ABOUT THE AUTHOR		viii
CONVERSION TABLES		x
Chapter 1	NEWCASTLE	1
Chapter 2	BROWNIES	19
Chapter 3	NIGHT 15	25
Chapter 4	FRIENDS AND NEIGHBOURS	33
Chapter 5	SHETLAND	51
Chapter 6	WALKERS' GROUP	69
Chapter 7	WORK	75
Chapter 8	THE USA	86
Chapter 9	INTERNATIONAL	19
Chapter 10	FAMILY FAVOURITES	114
EPILOGUE		120
INDEX		121

FOREWORD

THIS book was written to support Maternity Worldwide in saving lives in childbirth. It is primarily a recipe book, but it follows the pathway of my life and people I have met along the way. Maternity Worldwide is a registered charity with the aim of reducing the huge global toll of maternal death during childbirth. More than 99% of these deaths occur in developing countries. Everyone who contributed a recipe has already donated to Maternity Worldwide and all proceeds from the book will be given to the Charity.

Currently women in the poorest countries in the world have a high chance of dying in pregnancy or childbirth. In some parts of Africa this risk is as high as 1 in 7. Maternal death affect hundreds of thousands of families and communities. Millions of children are left motherless each year and globally an estimated 1 million babies die soon after the deaths of their mothers. But we can do something about it because relatively inexpensive treatments and access to obstetric care could save the lives of the great majority of these mothers and babies. Please look at the Maternity Worldwide website (www.maternityworldwide.org) and become a regular donor if you are able to.

So my 'recipe for life' is not just a cookbook drawing from family, friends and colleagues in my own life but, with the help of readers, it is also a very practical way of contributing to saving the lives of many hundreds and maybe thousands of people in other parts of the world.

In the recipes, I have resisted the temptation to standardise all of the units of measure. Some of the recipes are quite old, from several generations ago, and to have converted them all into modern day units would have meant losing something of their authenticity. For each recipe, I have therefore included first the units provided by the contributor, followed by a conversion into either traditional or metric units as appropriate. A conversion table is also included, so that readers can use whichever units of measure they prefer.

In requesting recipes, I did not specify starter, main course, dessert etc but, interestingly, when they came in, there was a good balance between the different types of recipe. There is no division of types of recipe within the text, but I have included sub-divisions within the index, which should make it easier to search.

The recipes have been obtained from family and many different friends. A very wide variety of recipes was received and I have included at least one from everyone. A big thank you to everyone who has contributed.

Anne Brown
Burley-in-Wharfedale
June 2006

ACKNOWLEDGEMENTS

WITHOUT the help of family and many friends, this book could never have been written. From the very first, the idea of putting together such a book in support of Maternity Worldwide received much encouragement and no-one dismissed it as 'just another impractical idea which would never come to fruition'. Of course, the real authors are those who supplied the recipes. Everyone put a great deal of effort into their selection with much digging into old family recipe books and producing recipes which were just a little different from those readily available. Recipes were received by letter, by e-mail, by hand, by telephone and collected over a period of two years in many different locations. Apologies are due if any went astray during this process and therefore do not appear in the book.

Special thanks are due to Stella Murdoch who kindly reviewed all of the recipes and helped to make them consistent and to Lauren Bulter who created the beautiful line drawings for Chapter 5. Many others have helped in the various stages of production of the book, especially with proof-reading and advice on format and their contribution is most gratefully acknowledged.

ABOUT THE AUTHOR

ANNE BROWN had the idea for this book in late 2002, when she first became fully aware of the scale of the problem of mothers dying during childbirth in certain developing countries. This was at the time when her son, Adrian, and several of his colleagues were establishing a new charity 'Maternity Worldwide' to help address the problem. Anne decided to write to all of her family and friends (enclosed with their Christmas cards) to ask for their help in supplying a favourite recipe or two, along with a donation. These recipes, along with Anne's own narrative and anecdotes, would form the basis of a book, which she had already decided would be called 'A Recipe for Life'.

The response from friends and family was overwhelming – almost everyone contacted supplied one or more recipes, along with interesting snippets on the origin of the recipes which came from more than 15 countries. The book soon began to take shape, but it also acted as the focus for much wider efforts to support Maternity Worldwide. Indeed, many of the people contacted to supply a recipe began to develop their own ideas on ways to raise support for the Charity. Money has been raised through coffee mornings, quizzes, sales, sponsored runs (including several marathons) and in a host of other ways.

But it was not just money which was raised. The Charity had begun its work in Western Ethiopia and Anne also had the idea of asking people (especially older ladies) to knit baby vests, as it can be quite cold at night in certain parts of Ethiopia. She obtained a pattern from a neighbour and began to distribute these. Before long, beautifully knitted vests started rolling in as shown in the photograph on page 37. This really caught on and expanded dramatically, so that vests were being made all over the UK. Clearly, this was also highly fulfilling for those who were doing the knitting.

The support from Anne and her family and friends helped to provide a foundation for the charity to become established and grow. Without such support, it may well have faltered. Many thousands of vests have now been made, along with knitted baby blankets, which are much appreciated in Ethiopia.

Anne had planned to go out to Ethiopia in October 2005 to visit the Charity's projects but, in July 2005, she became ill with cancer. She was determined to continue work on the book, although this became increasingly difficult. Nevertheless, she gathered in all of the recipes and completed the writing in June 2006 and was able to read and correct the first full draft of the manuscript. Sadly, Anne died in July 2006, having completed the book, but not having seen it in its final form.

So in many ways this book is a fitting memorial to Anne. Those who read the book will have no difficulty in perceiving what was her personal 'recipe for life'. She was always interested in people and their welfare, wherever they came from and whatever their 'station' in life. She made friends easily and often for life. She spent decades leading young people, both as a teacher and in out of school activities, such as the Brownie movement. She had a wonderful sense of humour, which surfaces now and then in the book. Above all, she was a loving, supportive and loyal wife, mother and friend.

CONVERSION TABLES

OVEN TEMPERATURES

°C	°F	Gas Mark
140	285	1
150	300	2
170	335	3
180	350	4
190	375	5
200	400	6
220	425	7
230	450	8
240	465	9

WEIGHTS

OUNCES	GRAMS
1	25
2	50
3	80
4	110
5	150
6	175
7	200
8	225
9	250
10	275
11	315
12	350
13	375
14	400
15	425
16 (1 lb)	450

VOLUMES

FLUID OUNCES	MILLILITRES
1	25
2	50
3	80
4	110
5	150
6	175
7	200
8	225
9	250
0	275
15	425
20 (1 pint)	570
25 (1¼ pints)	725
30 (1½ pints)	850
35 (1¾ pints)	1000 (1 litre)
40 (2 pints)	1,150

CHAPTER 1
NEWCASTLE

I WAS BORN the eldest of three sisters in Newcastle upon Tyne during the Second World War, when food was rationed and fresh ingredients were often impossible to obtain. Substitutes such as powdered egg and dried milk were in regular use and long queues formed outside food shops for basic foods. However, my childhood memories were of better things, both my mother, Harriet, and grandmother, Sarah, were excellent cooks and I started my apprenticeship at an early age standing on a chair to stir the mixtures. The scarcity of food led to great ingenuity from the women (few men cooked in those days) and the meals they provided. If an ingredient was not available, they cleverly substituted another. My Grandmother's handwritten workbook shows many examples of this ingenuity, including (surprisingly) how she substituted a tablespoonful of vinegar for one of the eggs in a cake recipe.

In those days, the main meal was usually eaten at midday and most people went home to eat it. After work in the evening, high tea was the usual offering which often consisted of cold meat, pickles, bread and butter/margarine and, if you were lucky, cake or a scone. Fruit and vegetables were not as plentiful as they are today and tended to be only the home grown variety that were in season. I always loved my Grandmother's first green salad of the season served with her home made dressing which was quite delicious, if a bit unusual. It is certainly worth trying.

SARAH'S CHOPPED GREEN SALAD AND DRESSING

Serves 4

½ plain round lettuce
¼ cucumber
1 bunch scallions (spring onions)
Tomato slices to garnish and/or hard boiled egg
1 tbsp milk
1 tsp vinegar
1 tsp sugar

Prepare dressing in a small basin by thoroughly mixing the milk, vinegar and sugar and add a pinch of salt.
　Finely shred the lettuce and chop the cucumber into small dice and the scallions into small circles. Mix well together and pour the dressing over the greens. Toss the salad in the dressing and garnish with tomato or egg slices and serve immediately. When serving, use a straining spoon to remove excess dressing. This salad is particularly good with home boiled ham or mince and onion tart.

As we lived in my Grandmother's home until I was 6 years old, she did most of the cooking, but my mother did have a few specialities of her own which included rabbit pie, sandwich cake, trifle and broth in the days when marrow bones for the stock were easily obtainable from your local butcher.

Nowadays, it is usually not possible to obtain the bones for the stock, so you will need to prepare some beef stock by stewing some beef with onions and straining off the liquor. In the old days, the vegetables for the broth were usually put through the hand-operated mincing machine, screwed to the kitchen table and this was fun to do. I still have the old machine, but it is easier now to use a food processor.

HARRIET'S BROTH

Serves 8

2 - 3 carrots
½ swede
2 onions
2 parsnips
Handful pearl barley
Salt and pepper to season
Beef stock or consommé

Prepare the beef stock by stewing some beef with onions and straining off the liquor. You will need approximately 1-2 pints/600–1200 ml. Alternatively, it is possible to use beef consommé. Place the chopped vegetables and barley in the stock in a large (6 pint/3.5 litre) saucepan and add extra water to allow for swelling of the barley (to make the total volume approximately 4 pints/2.25 litres). Bring up to simmering point and cook until the vegetables are tender. Serve with thickly sliced white bread.

The familiar view of the bridges, Newcastle Upon Tyne.

I can remember going with my Grandfather on a Sunday morning to visit his mother who was in her 90s and lived with her youngest daughter, Prudie. He usually took a parcel of groceries for her. Prudie always bought Great Grandma's clothes and she would look at the latest purchase and say 'Yes, but is it fashionable Prudie?' It seemed that, even in her nineties, she had to be in fashion. On the way back, we would stop off at the allotments and usually come home with a bunch of flowers and some mint for making mint sauce.

I loved being asked to make the mint sauce – stand on a chair and chop away. Grandma had a special cutter with many circular blades and you just pushed the small machine over the mint until it was chopped fine (and I use the same cutter to this day).

SARAH'S MINT SAUCE

2 tbsp fresh mint leaves (stalks removed)
1 tbsp sugar
1 tbsp water
2 tbsp vinegar

Finely chop the mint. Pour the sugar and water into a saucepan and boil for 1 minute. Add the vinegar and pour over the chopped mint. Soak for 15 minutes or until cool. Stir before serving.

After we moved from my Grandmother's house to our new home a few streets away, I soon made friends with another six-year old, Margaret, and we became inseparable playmates. We have been close ever since, and especially so in recent years. She and her husband, Ian, moved to Sheffield many years ago, but we see each other regularly. Margaret would not claim to be a great cook and her husband Ian has provided his recipe for curry, which he claims he brought from Newcastle to Yorkshire.

IAN'S GEORDIE CURRY

Serves 4

½-1 lb/225–450 g left-over cooked lamb, beef or chicken
1 large onion
1-2 cloves garlic
1 cooking apple
1 large carrot and/or parsnip
1 oz/25 g sultanas or raisins
2 tbsp vegetable or olive oil
1 tbsp curry powder (mild/med/hot) to taste
1 pint/570 ml chicken stock or water
Salt and pepper

Chop the garlic and onion and fry in oil until golden. Add diced carrot/parsnip and continue to fry for a few minutes before adding the chopped apple and sultanas or raisins. Cook for 5 minutes over a medium heat and then add the diced meat and continue to heat. When hot, add the curry powder stirring constantly to avoid burning. Add the chicken stock or water and season to taste with salt and pepper. Cook over a low/medium heat for ½ -1 hour (the longer the better). Do not allow to dry and add more stock or water if needed.

Curry is best cooked and refrigerated until the next day to improve the flavour, but this is not necessary.

Serve with boiled patna rice, popadoms and lime or mango chutney.

Whilst growing up in Newcastle, I was a pupil at Heaton High School (girls only). This was built on one side of a high wall and on the other side was a mirror image school (the boys' school). It is hard to imagine nowadays, but there was almost no mixing of the schools (at least not officially) – no joint lessons and certainly no joint social activities. One of my best friends at school was Christine. After school, she moved south to take up nursing and I have only seen her once in the last 45 years. However, we have kept in regular touch and she sent me these recipes. Christine's Barbecued Spare Ribs is a favourite of hers and she says: *'This dish freezes well and will reheat well in the sauce'*. For Pear Belle Helene, Christine says: *'This is a quick and easy dessert to prepare, but tastes delicious'*.

CHRISTINE'S BARBECUED SPARE RIBS

Serves 4

Spare ribs of pork cut into 4 thick chops
$1/2$ oz/12 g butter or 1 tbsp cooking oil
1 onion (peeled and chopped)
1 stick of celery (washed and chopped)
1 courgette (washed and sliced)
A few mushrooms (sliced)
1 level tbsp brown sugar
2 level tsp dry mustard
1 level tsp salt
$1/2$ level tsp paprika pepper
$1^1/_2$ tbsp tomato paste
1 tbsp Worcester sauce
$1/4$ pint/140 ml water
1 tbsp vinegar
2 tbsp lemon juice

Mix the sugar, mustard, salt and pepper with the tomato paste and add the liquids. Place the chops in a wide shallow casserole dish and bake uncovered at 200°C/390°F/Gas Mark 6 for 30 minutes or until well browned. Pour off any fat. Meanwhile, fry the onion in the butter or oil until brown. Add the remaining ingredients and pour over the chops. Cover and bake for about $3/4$ hour.

Serve with mashed or baked jacket potatoes and green vegetables.

CHRISTINE'S PEAR BELLE HELENE

Serves 4

4 pears (fresh or canned)
Vanilla ice cream
Chocolate sauce
1 oz/25 g butter
1 level tbsp cocoa
1 generous tbsp golden syrup

Peel and quarter the pears and place in four individual dishes. For the chocolate sauce, add butter, cocoa and golden syrup to a pan or microwaveable dish. Heat just long enough to melt the butter, stirring all the time (this may be on the hob or a few seconds in the microwave).

To serve, place 2 scoops of ice cream on each dish of pears and drizzle the chocolate sauce over the ice cream.

This is a quick and easy dessert to prepare but tastes delicious.

A famous North-East landmark, St Mary's Island is accessible by causeway twice a day when the tide ebbs.

I joined the Girl Guides at Heaton Methodist Church in my early teens and that started what turned out to be decades of association with the Brownie and Guide movement. After Guides on a Friday evening, I remember tiptoeing up the stairs to peer in at the upper hall, where the Church Youth Club was being held. Around 40 young people were dancing and the girls were wearing colourful, circular skirts. Oh how I longed to be 15 and old enough to join. Gradually, in the late 1950s, Heaton Methodist Church became a major part of my life. I became a Guide leader, joined the Youth Club (which lived up to all my expectations) and became a member of the 'Youth Fellowship' which met after church on a Sunday evening. It was there that I met so many people that have become lifelong friends, including my husband, Stan, who I married at Heaton Methodist Church in 1963. Some of these friends have been kind enough to share their recipes for this book.

Along with my younger sister Jean, Joan Suggett was a bridesmaid at our wedding. She married my husband's best friend, Alan, so we were a close group (and still are). Here is Joan's recipe for Crème Brulée.

JOAN'S CRÈME BRULÉE

Serves 6

4 egg yolks
1 tbsp caster sugar
2 x 284 ml/10 fl oz cartons double cream
A few drops vanilla essence

To finish
50 g/2 oz caster sugar

Beat the egg yolks and sugar together. Warm the double cream in a saucepan or bowl over a pan of simmering water. Carefully stir in the egg mixture. Continue cooking gently, stirring constantly until thickened (enough to coat the back of a spoon). Add the vanilla essence.

Strain into 6 ramekin dishes and place in a roasting pan, containing 2.5 cm/ 1 inch of water. Place in a pre-heated oven 140°C/280°F/Gas Mark 1, for 30 – 40 minutes. Remove the dishes from the pan, cool then chill in refrigerator overnight.

To finish

Sprinkle evenly with sugar. Place under the grill until the sugar has caramelised (or use blow torch if available). Chill in refrigerator for approximately 2 hours to set, and serve.

As an extra, sliced raspberries or strawberries can be placed in the ramekin dishes before filling.

Joan's sister Rosemarie and her husband Keith have also been good friends for many years. Rosemarie has given me this rich traditional recipe for Tiramisu and another friend from those days, Jennifer Stephenson, has provided a recipe for Chicken and Mushroom Lasagne.

ROSEMARIE'S TIRAMISU

Serves 6

1 packet sponge fingers
3 tbsp strong black coffee
3 – 5 tbsp amaretto
3 egg yolks
2 oz/50 g caster sugar
8 oz/225 g cream cheese (Philadelphia)
1 oz/25 g roasted almonds
Whipped cream
Cocoa powder

Rapidly dip the sponge fingers into black coffee and place in a trifle dish. Scatter in the amaretto. Whip egg yolks, sugar and cream cheese together and spread over the sponge base. Cool in refrigerator for at least 1 hour. Whip the cream and spread over, and then scatter with cocoa powder and roasted almonds.

Jennifer says 'At our church we regularly have Parish lunch together and when it was our Home Group's turn to do the catering, we served this recipe for 80 people. It was a huge success – at least everyone said they liked it – and as a Home Group we had fun preparing it. The men were in charge of the nutmeg and cheese grating and garlic chopping (yes, there were some sore knuckles) and we women were very good at the stirring'.

JENNIFER'S CHICKEN AND MUSHROOM LASAGNE

Serves 6-8.

12 oz/350 g skinless chicken breast fillets
Salt and pepper
2 large cloves garlic (chopped)
2 oz/50 g plain flour (sieved)
8 oz/225 g mature cheddar cheese (grated)
6 oz/175 g sliced mushrooms
2 oz/50 g breadcrumbs
1 tsp vegetable oil
2 oz/50 g butter
¼ whole nutmeg (grated)
2 pints/1,100 ml milk
1 tbsp wholegrain mustard
8 oz/225 g lasagne
3 tbsp grated parmesan cheese

Preheat the oven to 190°C/375°F/Gas Mark 5. Season the chicken, then rub with oil and bake in an oven-proof dish for 25-30 minutes until cooked. Chop into small pieces.

Meanwhile, melt the butter in a saucepan over medium heat. Add the chopped garlic and stir for 1 minute. Add the grated nutmeg and remove from the heat. Add the sieved flour and stir until smooth. Add the milk, a little at a time, stirring well, return the saucepan to the heat and bring to the boil, stirring constantly. Allow to simmer for 2 to 3 minutes. Add the grated cheese and wholegrain mustard. Remove from the heat and season to taste. Halve the sauce, add the sliced mushrooms and chicken to one half and reserve the remainder.

Lightly grease a large lasagne dish and arrange alternate layers of lasagne and the chicken and mushroom sauce, ending with a lasagne layer. Top with the reserved cheese sauce and scatter over breadcrumbs and grated parmesan.

To cook, reduce the oven temperature to 180°C/350°F/Gas Mark 4 and bake in the centre of the oven for about 40 minutes until golden brown. Serve with green salad and crusty bread.

Stan's mother, Ruth, was popular for her chocolate cake and her sisters Marjorie and Dorothy for their 'Singing Hinnies' and 'Maids of Honour'. Although Marjorie and Dorothy did not live in Newcastle, we visited them most weeks in Easington Lane, near Durham, where they lived and looked after Stan's Grandma, who had been crippled from her early 40s, when she fell between a ship (her husband was a seaman) and the quayside. Her husband died in an accident at sea soon afterwards, so the family had a tough time. Marjorie was unmarried and a District Nurse all of her working life, but she also did much other unpaid work in her mining community, as well as unstinting work for the Red Cross. These recipes are not original to them, but they bring back happy memories of our visits to their homes.

RUTH'S CHOCOLATE CAKE

4 tbsp margarine
4 tbsp sugar
4 tbsp SR flour
1 tbsp cocoa
4 eggs

Beat together the margarine and the sugar, add the SR flour, the cocoa and 4 eggs and mix well. Turn into a well greased cake tin and bake for 45 minutes at 180°C/350°F/Gas Mark 4.

Cut the cake into two layers and make the butter icing for placing between the layers with an additional 2 tbsp margarine and icing sugar, well mixed. Make the chocolate icing for the top of the cake with cocoa to taste, icing sugar and a small amount of water.

DOROTHY'S SINGING HINNIES

8 oz/225 g plain flour
4 oz/110 g butter
1 level tsp baking powder
Pinch salt
3 tbsp currants
¼ pint/150 ml whole milk

Mix the flour, baking powder and salt and rub in the butter, but leave the butter in tiny lumps. Add the currants and mix with the milk to a rather wet scone consistency. Divide into 6 parts and roll into balls in your hands, using plenty of flour, then roll each out into a thin, roughly round shape and cook on a griddle until golden brown. When the little lumps of butter bubble through the mix and sizzle, the singing sound is heard.

The Singing Hinnies are best served hot as scones, with butter and jam.

MARJORIE'S MAIDS OF HONOUR

Makes about 25 small pastry cakes
12 oz/350 g SR flour
2 oz/50 g lard
4 oz/110 g margarine
½ tsp salt
3 oz/80 g sugar
2 tbsp milk
1 egg

For the pastry, mix the salt and 8 oz/225 g flour. Rub in the lard and 2 oz/50 g margarine lightly until the mix is like bread crumbs. Stir in 1 oz/25 g sugar and mix with cold water to a stiff dough.

Prepare the cake mixture by beating 2 oz/50 g sugar and 2 oz/50 g margarine to a 'cream' in a warm basin. Beat the egg with the milk and then stir in 4 oz/110 g flour and the beaten egg into the cream alternately, a little at a time. Mix thoroughly.

Roll the pastry out thinly and cut into rounds with a scone cutter. Line small patty tins with the pastry, add a little jam to each, then 1 tsp of the cake mixture. Bake in a hot oven at 220°C/430°F/Gas Mark 7 for about 20 minutes.

My sister-in-law, Heather, has catered for many family parties and one of the favourites is this recipe for toffee cake. It is delicious, but very rich. Heather says *'I have always called this Toffee Cake, although it sometimes is called Caramel Crumble. I always made one of these to take on self-catering holidays when my boys were young. So when one of these appeared, it was a sure sign that we were going somewhere. I had usually bought a large tin of condensed milk, so a second Toffee Cake usually appeared soon after our return'*.

HEATHER'S TOFFEE CAKE

For this recipe, first make the crumble and then the toffee, before combining them.

Crumble
4 oz/110 g margarine
1 level tsp baking powder
2 oz/50 g caster sugar
6 oz/175 g plain flour

Cream the sugar and margarine and then add the flour and baking powder. Knead well. Press mixture into a Swiss-roll tin and bake at 180°C/350°F/Gas Mark 4 until light brown.

Toffee
4 oz/110 g margarine
1 tbsp syrup
4 oz/110 g sugar
1 small tin condensed milk

Melt all of the ingredients into a pan, bring to the boil and boil for 5 minutes, stirring constantly. Spread this mixture onto the crumble and leave to cool. Melt 4 oz/110 g cooking chocolate and spread over.

Whilst we were living in Newcastle, our first child, Janet, was born. That same week, Hovis Bread was having a special event. To match their slogan 'Don't just say Brown, say Hovis', any family with the surname 'Brown', having a new-born baby that week would be given free Hovis bread every day for 13 months (a baker's dozen). One of our friends had alerted us to this offer. As you can imagine, a loaf of bread every day can be too much but, fortunately, the manager of the baker's shop allowed us to substitute cream cakes for any unclaimed bread at the end of each week. Quite a treat! For the next recipe (one of my own), you can use Hovis (or any other make of brown bread).

ANNE'S BROWN BREAD ICE CREAM

Makes about 750 ml/1¼ pints ice cream

45 g/2 oz wholemeal breadcrumbs
550 ml/1 pint whipping/double cream
180 g/6 oz demerara sugar
3 tbsp dark rum
¼ tsp vanilla extract

Spread the crumbs out evenly on a large baking tray and toast under the grill, turning them at short intervals so that they brown evenly. Measure the cream into a jug and stir in the cooled, browned crumbs and the remaining ingredients; cover and chill for 1 hour to give the crumbs a chance to soften.
When ready, either still freeze or start an ice-cream machine, giving the mix a good stir before pouring it into the machine. Churn until the mixture has the consistency of softly whipped cream. Now quickly scrape into plastic freezer boxes and cover with a piece of waxed or greaseproof paper and a lid.
Finally label and place in the freezer. Once firmly frozen, it will need about 30 minutes in the refrigerator before it is soft enough to serve.

More recently, my sister, Jean, moved house and she and her husband, Dave, have become keen gardeners. This is her recipe for summer pudding, which she makes with all of her own fruit. Jean says *'I like this recipe because I acquired a large garden that was well stocked with fruit trees and bushes. I needed recipes to use up the fruit and this is so easy to make, yet looks quite impressive'*.

JEAN'S SUMMER PUDDING

Serves 6 – 8

8 oz/225 g redcurrants
4 oz/110 g blackcurrants
1 lb/450 g raspberries
5 oz/150 g sugar
7 – 8 medium slices white bread
from a large uncut loaf

Clean and wash all the fruit, cover with the sugar and cook in a large saucepan for 3 – 5 minutes until the sugar melts.

Remove the pan from the heat and line a pudding basin (850 ml/1½ pint, lightly greased) with bread, making sure there are no gaps. Reserve about two-thirds of a cupful of the juice and keep refrigerated to touch up the pudding the next day.

Pour the fruit and remaining juice into the lined basin and make a lid with the last slice of bread. Weigh down the pudding with a saucer and something heavy on top and keep in the refrigerator overnight.

To serve, turn out on a large dish or plate and brush over any of the bread that still looks white with the spare juice. Cut into wedges and serve with thick cream. You can garnish with a sprig of mint if desired.

This pudding freezes quite well and can also be made into small individual puddings (see through yogurt pots work well).

Jean's sister-in-law, Irene, makes a delicious mushroom soup and I could not resist including it here.

IRENE'S CREAM OF MUSHROOM SOUP

Serves 4-6

225 g/8 oz mushrooms
80 g/3 oz butter
175 g/6 oz onions, skinned & chopped
40 g/1½ oz plain flour
900 ml / 1½ pints chicken stock
300 ml/½ pint milk
Salt & pepper
A pinch of garlic salt
Lemon juice.

Remove stalks from mushrooms and slice the mushroom caps thinly. Melt the butter in a large saucepan and sauté the mushroom caps until just tender. Remove from the pan with a slotted spoon and reserve.

In the remaining butter, sauté the onions until tender, stir in the flour and cook for 3 minutes, continuing to stir. Slowly add stock stirring all of the time. Bring to the boil and simmer gently for 20 minutes. Cool the mixture and purée in a blender until smooth.

Return the mixture to the saucepan, add milk, salt and pepper, garlic salt, and lemon juice to taste. Simmer for 10 minutes. Return the reserved mushroom slices to the soup and heat.

Serve immediately with croutons if desired.

My niece Valerie is a Home Economics teacher. She has two young boys, so I am now a great aunt. Valerie has contributed the following two recipes. Valerie says 'The recipe for praline cake was passed on to me by a good friend and colleague who has just retired at the age of 71. I have used it with several cookery classes and it is always a great success'.

VAL'S CHICKEN AND ASPARAGUS BAKE

Serves 4

4 chicken breasts cooked
425g/1 lb can of asparagus spears
485g/1 lb can of creamy chicken & corn soup
½ cup of soured cream
2 spring onions sliced diagonally
1 medium red pepper thinly sliced
Salt and black pepper
1 cup of cheddar cheese, grated
½ cup of parmesan cheese, grated
½ tsp of sweet paprika.

Heat the oven to 180°C/350°F/Gas Mark 4. Slice the chicken finely and line a large ovenproof dish with chicken. Top with half of the asparagus. Combine the soup, soured cream, spring onions and red pepper. Season to taste and pour over the chicken.

Arrange the remaining asparagus on top and cover with both cheeses. Sprinkle with paprika, bake for 30 minutes and serve.

VAL'S PRALINE CAKE

4 oz/110 g butter or margarine
4 oz/110 g sugar
2 oz/50 g coconut
2 oz/50 g ground almonds
2 oz/50 g SR flour, sieved
1 large chocolate milk flake
2 eggs
1 drop of almond essence
1 small bar of milk chocolate (optional)

Cream the fat and sugar together. Beat the eggs and add the essence. Add this to the creamed fat and sugar. Add all other ingredients except the chocolate and stir well.

Crumble the flake and add to the mixture. Bake the mixture in a 7 inch/18 cm cake tin, at 170°C/340°F/Gas Mark 3 for 1 hour. When cool, if required, spread melted milk chocolate on top.

My daughter Janet met her friends Sue and Trina when they were all at University of Newcastle together and they have kindly donated these recipes.

SUE'S SLOE GIN

1 lb/450 g sloe berries
1 pint/570 ml gin
4 oz/110 g caster sugar

The above quantities should be adjusted according to the volume of sloe gin required. Sloes are the purplish berries which are the fruit of the blackthorn bushes, found in many country hedgerows. They should be collected in autumn and then need to be pierced or placed in the freezer when they will burst on thawing.

Place the pierced sloes in a bottle with the gin and sugar and shake daily for the first few weeks. Filter after 3 months, when the sloe gin should appear a deep ruby red. It can then be drunk, but is best left to mature for up to one year.

If desired, the flavour can be enhanced by adding $\frac{1}{4}$ oz almonds or 2 cloves at the bottling stage.

Sloe gin can be enjoyed hot or cold.

SUE'S MACKEREL PATÉ

Serves 6

12 oz/350 g smoked mackerel
Juice of 1 orange
1 tbsp lemon juice
4 oz/110 g cottage cheese
150 ml/$\frac{1}{4}$ pint natural yoghurt
1 small clove garlic
$\frac{1}{4}$ tsp mace
Salt and pepper to taste

Carefully skin and bone the mackerel and discard. Add the mackerel and all ingredients to a food processor and mix thoroughly. The paté is ready to serve.

TRINA'S BABI KETCHUP

Serves 4-6

2 lb/900 g pork fillet
2 oz/50 g oil
2 tsp ground ginger
³/₄ tsp chilli
1 or 2 cloves garlic, crushed or chopped
2 onions, chopped
½ pint/275 ml stock
1 tbsp soft brown sugar
1 tbsp lemon juice
2 tbsp soy
Salt and pepper
Cornflour

Make cubes of the pork and fry to brown and seal the surfaces. Remove the pork, fry the onions and add pepper (to taste), garlic, ginger, chilli and soy. Add the stock, sugar and lemon juice.

Stir in the fried pork and simmer for approximately 20-30 minutes. It can be thickened with cornflour, stirred into cold water if required. Adjust the seasoning to personal preferences.

Serve with boiled rice and squeaky beans (or whatever you fancy really).

Another of Janet's friends, Sarah, is a keen camper and has given this recipe. She says *'after a hard day's walking you need food that is easy to cook and preferably only using one pan. I use a Trangia, a methylated spirit stove that has slightly longer cooking times than most of the gas alternatives'*.

SARAH'S WALKERS' REVIVAL

Serves 2

Pasta for two
1 packet pasta sauce
1 tin tuna
1 tin sweetcorn

Cook the pasta in boiling water for about 15 minutes. Drain off excess water and add the tuna and sweetcorn. Cook for a further 15 minutes. Serve, sit back and eat whilst hopefully enjoying a wonderful view.

CHAPTER 2
BROWNIES

WHILST in Newcastle, I became leader (Brown Owl) of the Church Brownie Guide Pack until we went to live in America, when my sister took my place. On our return, when we moved to Leeds in 1971, Adel Methodist Church was appealing for someone to run the Brownie Pack and so began my time as Brown Owl at Adel. Although I retired from Brownies some ten years ago, I have kept in touch with many of my ex-Brownies, who now have a host of different careers and fulfilling lives. The following are some recipes from girls who were in my Brownie Pack at Adel Methodist Church in Leeds.

CLARE'S CHICKEN IN RED PESTO SAUCE

Serves 4

3 tbsp olive oil
4 chicken breasts
200 ml/7 fl oz crème fraiche (half fat)
400 ml /14 fl oz can chopped tomatoes
3 tbsp red pesto
Salt and pepper
Black olives
Basil leaves

Heat the oil in an oven proof dish and add the chicken breasts (whole or diced) and brown quickly on both sides.
    Mix together the crème fraiche, tomatoes and pesto. Pour this mixture over the chicken and place in the oven at 200°C/400°F/Gas Mark 6 for 35-45 min, depending on the size of the chicken pieces. Season, sprinkle over the basil and black olives and serve.

RUTH'S AVOCADO, BACON AND PINE NUT SALAD

This is a very simple recipe, ideal for lunchtime visitors. It is best served with a good chutney and some warm ciabatta bread.

Serves 4

Mixed salad leaves – preferably containing rocket and watercress for flavour
1 large avocado.
4 slices smoked bacon (or proscuitto ham)
1 handful of pine nuts
Drizzle of olive oil or herb oil

Prepare the avocado by cutting it in half, removing the stone with a knife and dividing the flesh into squares. Cut around the skin edge to remove. Mix the salad leaves in a bowl. Grill the bacon until crispy.

Add the avocado squares to the salad and drizzle with the oil. Lightly roast the pine nuts in a frying pan with no oil. Just keep moving them around the pan until brown. Cut up the bacon into 1 cm strips and add to the salad, before placing the pine nuts on top.

ALISON'S EGG FREE TIRAMISU

397g/14 oz can of sweetened condensed milk
450 g/1 lb Mascarpone cheese
3 tbsp Marsala wine or brandy
150 ml/¼ pint cold, strong, black coffee
110 g/4 oz sponge fingers
2 tbsp cocoa powder

Beat together the condensed milk and mascarpone cheese.

In a shallow dish, mix the alcohol with the coffee. Take one sponge finger at a time and dip it into the coffee mixture, holding it for a few seconds whilst taking care not to let it become soggy. Line a trifle dish with half the dipped sponge fingers. Spoon over half the milk and cheese mixture. Sift over a generous dusting of cocoa.

Repeat with another layer of dipped sponge fingers, milk and cheese mixture and dusting of cocoa.

Chill for at least 30 minutes before serving. (Can be prepared a day ahead and stored in the refrigerator).

More than 30 years as a Brownie leader has left me with many memories of happy times. I especially remember the fun we had at Pack Holidays. One year in particular, we were short-staffed and a Brownie mum offered to come and help. When she asked if she should bring her parachute, I was a little surprised but agreed to it. What a great time the Brownies had playing with that parachute – it was the highlight of the weekend.

But being a Brownie leader and looking after 7 – 10 year old girls is not all as genteel as you might think. Let me tell you about a particularly rounders match which would put some modern football aggression into the shade. That year, around 1985, the District Meeting had decided to hold a rounders knock-out competition to improve the competitive team spirit of the girls. As I was coaching an eleven year old rounders team at School, I though it might be a good idea to enter our Brownie Pack for the competition. All went well at first and we progressed through the early rounds until the night of the semi-finals, which was to prove one of the most unforgettable nights of my life. Our team was doing really well and we had not played our reserve. Suddenly, I saw storming towards me, the mother of our reserve who was puce in the face. She was so angry that her daughter had not yet been played and I had to suffer 10 minutes of abuse whilst trying at the same time to encourage the team. Just as this incident was drawing to a close, a delegation of parents from the opposing team approached us and accused our best player of being a boy. I don't know what they expected me to do to disprove this and I called upon her mum to 'vouch' for her, but I'm not sure this was totally convincing because the mum's name was Terry. The last straw came when the opposition was batting and their fathers started encouraging their team to hurl their bats at my team instead of carrying them around the bases as required by the rules. Although we won the match it was memorable for all the wrong reasons and when I arrived home that evening I was still trembling.

I often went on trainings and whilst at Waddow (a Guide and Brownie Centre in Lancashire), I came across this recipe for Chocolate Surprise Pudding.

ANNE'S CHOCOLATE SURPRISE PUDDING

Serves 6

3 oz/80 g SR Flour
Pinch salt
2 tbsp cocoa
4 oz/110 g margarine
4 oz/110 g sugar
2 eggs
½ tsp vanilla essence
2 tbsp milk

Sauce
4 oz/110 g soft brown sugar
2 tbsp cocoa dissolved in ½ pint/275 ml hot water

Cream the margarine and sugar, add the beaten egg, then flour and 2 tbsp cocoa. Stir in the vanilla and milk. Spread the mixture into an 8 in/20 cm Pyrex dish.

Separately, add the brown sugar to the cocoa – water mixture and stir until the sugar has dissolved. Pour this sauce on top of the pudding mixture. Stand in a shallow dish with 1 inch/2.5 cm cold water to cook at 180°C/350°F/ Gas Mark 4 for 45 minutes to 1 hour.

To conclude, here are two more recipes from my Adel Brownies, sisters, Ruth and Helen. For the Banana Sponge Cake, Ruth says *'This recipe is loved by all ages and is great on a winter's evening. It also looks good and is very easy'.*

RUTH'S BANANA SPONGE CAKE

Serves 6

Butter to grease 20 cm/8 in cake tin
80 g/3 oz butter
5 bananas, sliced
4 tbsp caster sugar
2 tbsp water

Sponge
3 eggs (medium)
80 g/3 oz caster sugar
80 g/3 oz plain flour

Grease the cake tin and line with greaseproof paper. Preheat the the oven to 190°C/375°F Gas Mark 5. Melt half the butter, add the sliced bananas and cook in a saucepan for 2 minutes until soft and starting to brown. Put the mixture into the bottom of the cake tin. Dissolve the 4 tbsp sugar in water in a frying pan and simmer until it starts to caramelise. Add the remaining butter and pour over the bananas.

For the sponge, whisk the eggs and sugar together until stiff enough to draw a line across the surface of the mixture. Sift the flour and fold in. Pour the mixture over the bananas and bake for 30 – 35 minutes. Invert onto a serving dish and serve hot with custard.

For Helen's Perfect Pizzas, she says *'my children Luke and Annabel love to throw the dough and flatten it out. They also very good at helping to eat the Pizzas'*

HELEN'S PERFECT PIZZAS

Serves 4

8 oz/225 g plain flour
1 tsp salt
2 tsp easy blend dried yeast
1 can of tomatoes
1 tbs tomato puree
1tsp oregano
4 oz/110 g grated cheese
4 oz/110 g mushrooms
(other toppings e.g. ham and pineapple)

Sieve the flour and salt into a bowl. Mix in the yeast and sufficient warm water to make a soft ball of dough. Place the dough onto a floured surface and knead for 5 minutes. Place the dough in a greased bowl, cover and leave in a warm place for 1 hour.

When the dough has doubled in size, knead it again for 5 minutes and divide it into 4 equal balls. Place the balls on a greased baking tray and flatten them out. Preheat the oven to 230°C/ 450°F/Gas Mark 8.

Sieve the tomatoes into a bowl, add the puree and salt and pepper and spread this mixture on the 4 pizza bases. Add the desired toppings and bake for 20-30 minutes.

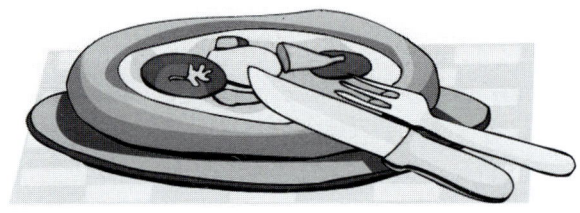

CHAPTER 3
NIGHT 15

STAN was appointed to an academic position at the University of Leeds and we moved on New Years Day 1971, when Janet was nearly two years old. The house we were proposing to buy had been withdrawn from the market because the owner had suffered a major fire in his carpet store – at least that was the reason given, we never did work out the connection. We had sold our lovely home in Newcastle and so had to find urgent accommodation in Leeds. We lived in a University student bed sit for a week or two, but then had the chance to rent a brand new council maisonette in Hunslet, South Leeds. This seemed too good an opportunity to miss. Apparently, Hunslet in the old days had been a really close knit community but the 'visionary' council had decided that everyone should be re-housed in medium-rise concrete blocks with modern amenities. The accommodation itself was fine (apart from the fact that there wasn't a single tree or blade of grass to be seen anywhere), but it was a little scary in the first week when a murder happened in a neighbouring flat and the police came round and warned everyone to keep their doors locked. Anyhow, the housing project failed utterly, the community never re-established itself and the buildings were demolished after just 15 years.

After 6 months in Hunslet, we moved to a new house in Holt Park, Adel, North Leeds. This was another experiment in social housing, in which a new village centre was created, with private housing, council housing and housing association accommodation built around the centre. At this time, we joined Adel Methodist Church, where we were to stay for 20 years. There were many young families at the church and in the area, but little social activity. With Margaret and Stephen Peacock, we started a group called 'Night 15', so-called because the plan was to meet on the 15th of every month. That way, the group would meet on different days of the week, so that no-one with fixed weekly commitments would be ruled out. The group has been a great success and is still going strong, although the members have grown older with the group. It has done a great deal of good work in the area and has been a vital force in the Church. We still meet around the 15th of every month and have a very varied social programme. We have had medieval banquets, canal trips, hiking weekends and a great deal of fun over the years. I still smile when I think of our very first meeting 'The Kick Off', when everyone came dressed as footballers or supporters.

Through Night 15, I have made many close friends and here are some of their recipes.

Cherrie Dacre says of Elsie Stott's Fruit Cake *'This is my favourite fruit cake recipe. It makes a good Christmas cake if you prefer one that isn't too rich. The recipe came from Elsie Stott, a contemporary of my Granny's, famous in the small Lancashire village in which they lived for her cakes and pastries'.*

ELSIE STOTT'S FRUIT CAKE

8 oz/225 g self-raising flour
6 oz/175 g butter
6 oz/175 g soft brown sugar
6 oz/175 g currants
6 oz/175 g raisins
4 oz/110 g sultanas
2 oz/50 g cherries
2 oz/50 g ground almonds
3 eggs
1 tsp mixed spice
1 tsp golden syrup

Cream the butter and sugar then beat in the eggs. Fold in all other ingredients. Bake at 140°C/280°F/Gas Mark 1 for 1 hour then lower temperature slightly (about 2 hours in total).

GRACE'S CRUNCHY COCONUT BISCUITS

4 oz/110 g butter or margarine
4 oz/110 g sugar
4 oz/110 g SR flour
4 oz/110 g coconut

Soften the butter/margarine and cream with the sugar. Add the flour, then coconut and then thoroughly mix together. Roll into balls, then press out into biscuits. Cook at 180°C/350°F/Gas Mark 4 for about 15 minutes.

CYNTHIA'S MARYLAND COOKIES

3 oz/80 g margarine
3 oz/80 g caster sugar
4 oz/110 g SR flour
3 oz/80 g chopped chocolate

Beat the margarine and sugar together until creamed. Work in the flour. Add the small pieces of chocolate and mix well. Divide the mixture into about 20 small balls and place on a greased baking tray. Bake at 180°C/350°F/Gas Mark 4 for about 15 minutes.

NORMA'S MEDIEVAL PUDDING

Serves 4
¼ pint/150 ml double cream
8 fl oz/225 ml plain yoghurt
½ lemon rind grated (no juice)
2 oz/50 g DK Muscovado sugar
1 tsp Schwartz All Spice (may be called Jamaican Pepper)

This dish can either be prepared in a medium sized glass bowl or in coupe glasses. Whip the cream to a stylish mix. Stir in the rind and fold in the yoghurt. Mix the sugar and spice separately and assemble the pudding as follows.

Half fill the bowl (or coupe glasses) with half the cream and yoghurt mix. Spread half the sugar/spice on top. Continue to fill up with another cream and yoghurt mix layer and the remaining sugar and spice. Drag a knife across several times to form a herring bone-like pattern. Chill in the refrigerator for a minimum of two hours, but all day or overnight is better to develop the flavour.

Serve the finished dish with Ratafia biscuits (eg Amaretta biscuits) obtainable in two sizes (the smaller ones are daintier). It can be presented with a few almond thins for guests to help themselves.

DOROTHY'S SYLLABUB TRIFLE

8 trifle sponges
2 tbsp red jam or jelly
8 tbsp sweet sherry
8 oz/225 g redcurrants/cranberries
2 lb/900 g caster sugar
8 oz/225 g raspberries fresh or frozen)
1 lemon
½ pint/275 ml double cream

Split trifle sponges through the centre and spread with red jam or jelly. Arrange in a bowl and sprinkle half the sherry over. Put the cranberries or redcurrants in a pan with half the caster sugar and cook gently in their juices for 5 minutes. Remove from the heat, add the raspberries and mix together. Spoon over the sponges, reserving a few cranberries/redcurrants to decorate later. Leave to cool.

Put remaining sherry, caster sugar, the grated rind of the lemon and 1 tbsp lemon juice into a small bowl and leave to infuse for 30 minutes. Whip cream to form soft peaks and fold in sherry and lemon mix carefully. Spoon syllabub onto the fruit and sponge. Decorate with reserved fruit.

Finally, here are two three course meals from friends Mike Wheeler and Joan Stevenson.

MIKE'S THREE COURSE DINNER

Starter - Potted Prawns

Serves 4

Preparation time, 15 minutes; cooking time 15 minutes plus cooling time.
350 g/12 oz cooked peeled, prawns
225 g/8 oz butter
Cayenne pepper
Ground mace or grated nutmeg
Pepper
Hot toast to serve
Garnish: Crisp lettuce leaves and watercress sprigs

Pat the prawns dry with absorbent paper to remove as much excess moisture as possible. Melt half of the butter in a saucepan, add the prawns and heat them through slowly over low heat, tossing the pan occasionally. Season with a large pinch of Cayenne pepper and mace or nutmeg and pepper to taste. Divide the buttered prawns between four ramekins and leave to become quite cold. Gently melt the remaining butter and pour just enough over each ramekin to cover the prawns. Cool and store in the refrigerator until needed.

Line four serving plates with lettuce leaves, run a sharp knife around the edge of the ramekins and turn out on top. Garnish with lemon wedges and sprigs of watercress. Serve with triangles of hot toast.

MIKE'S THREE COURSE DINNER

Main Course – Crispy Topped Beef
Preparation time, 40 minutes; cooking time 2 hours

Serves 4

700 g/1½ lb braising steak, cut into 3 cm/1¼ inch cubes
2 onions, thinly sliced
1 garlic clove, crushed
2 tbsp flour
200 ml/7 fl oz red wine
2 bay leaves
600 ml/1 pint hot beef stock
110 g/4 oz frozen sweetcorn, defrosted
3 celery stalks, cut into 1 cm/½ in slices
Salt and pepper
Celery leaves to garnish
For the topping:
110 g/4 oz butter
225 g/8 oz breadcrumbs
175 g/6 oz cheddar cheese, grated

Heat 2 tbsp of oil in a large, flameproof casserole and fry the beef in batches until golden brown on all sides, adding more oil as needed. Remove the meat and keep warm. Add the onions and garlic to the casserole and fry for 3 – 4 minutes until the onions are just beginning to colour. Remove from the heat, stir in the flour and cook slowly for a few minutes. Add the beef, wine, bay leaves and enough stock to just cover the meat. Season, bring to the boil, cover and simmer very gently for about 1 hour.

Add the sweetcorn and celery to the casserole and continue to simmer very gently, while making the topping. Heat the oven to 180°C/350°F/Gas Mark 4.

To make the topping, melt the butter in a large frying pan, add the breadcrumbs and stir over medium heat until golden brown and all the butter has been absorbed. Mix the breadcrumbs with the grated cheese and spread evenly over the beef. Bake for 30 – 40 minutes or until the top is golden brown and crusty and the cheese has melted. Garnish with celery leaves and serve at once.

MIKE'S THREE COURSE DINNER

Dessert – Maracuja Mousse (Passion Fruit)

Serves 4 - 6

8 passion fruits
2 tins condensed milk
Same amount of double cream

Liquidise and de-seed the passion fruits and reserve the juice (also reserve one half a passion fruit). Liquidise the condensed milk and cream, add the juice and liquidize all three together. Put the mixture into a container and cover the top with the seeds and juice of the remaining half passion fruit. Freeze.

Remove from freer slightly before you require it. As an alternative, limes can be used (about 8) and grate the skin of a few to add rind to the mixture and on top.

JOAN'S THREE COURSE LUNCH

Starter - Cold Cucumber Soup

Serves 4

2 medium sized cucumbers
2 onions
200 ml/7 fl oz water
1 tbsp plain flour
25 g/1 oz butter
1 bay leaf
200 ml/7 fl oz stock
150 ml/5 fl oz single cream
Dill and chives, finely chopped
Grated lemon rind
Salt and pepper

Peel and slice the cucumbers and onions, reserving a few slices of cucumber as a garnish. Simmer in the water together with salt and pepper until soft. Liquidise. Melt the butter and stir in the flour, gradually adding the stock and stirring until it is smooth. Add the bay leaf and then the cucumber purée and simmer on a low heat, stirring to make it smooth. Add the cream, chopped herbs and lemon rind. Chill and garnish before serving.

JOAN'S THREE COURSE LUNCH

Main Course - Courgette Flan with Hawaiian Rice Salad

Serves 4

Courgette Flan
450 g/1 lb courgettes
110 g/4 oz cheddar cheese
280 ml/10 fl oz single cream
3 eggs
Salt and pepper
Shortcrust pastry

Make and roll out sufficient shortcrust pastry to line a 25 cm/12 inch flan dish. Bake blind in a moderately hot oven (200°C/400°F/Gas Mark 6) for 10 minutes. Remove from the oven and lower the temperature to 160°C/325°F/Gas Mark 3. Slice the courgettes as finely as possible and arrange in the flan dish. Grate the cheese finely and add the cream, eggs and seasoning, blending all together. Pour over the courgettes. Place in the oven for 30 minutes until set. Serve hot or cold.

Hawaiian Rice Salad
110 g/4 oz long-grain brown rice
4 tbsp French dressing
Half small pineapple
Half medium size green pepper
Salt and pepper to taste

Cook the rice in boiling water until tender – about 35 minutes. Drain and allow to cool, then toss in the French dressing. Dice the flesh from the pineapple. Chop the green pepper and add both to the rice. Season to taste.

The Lake District – frequently visited by 'Night 15'.

JOAN'S THREE COURSE LUNCH

Dessert - Frozen Apricot Mousse

Serves 4

250 g/9 oz dried apricots, soaked overnight in 450 ml/16 fl oz water
3 eggs, separated
80 g/3 oz soft brown sugar
280 ml/10 fl oz double cream

Put the apricots in a pan with their soaking water and simmer for 15 minutes, until softened. Drain, reserving the liquid. Cool slightly. Process the apricots to a purée, adding a little cooking liquid if necessary.

Whisk the egg yolks and the sugar until pale, add the apricot purée and blend well. Whisk the egg whites until stiff and fold into the purée. Then whip and fold in the double cream. Pour into a 1 litre freezer proof bowl, cover and seal and freeze until firm. Transfer to the refrigerator 30-50 minutes before serving to soften. Scoop into chilled dishes to serve.

CHAPTER 4
FRIENDS AND NEIGHBOURS

WE HAVE been very fortunate in our 'choice' of neighbours. When we were first married in 1963, we lived in a bungalow in Winlaton, County Durham, next door to Marion and Eric Evans and their growing family. We became firm friends. Marion now lives in Newcastle upon Tyne and we are still in regular contact. Her husband Eric was a well-known local artist and we still treasure two of his oil paintings of local coastal scenes.

MARION'S CHEDDERY COTTAGE PIE

Serves 4

12 oz /350 g minced beef
1 large onion (chopped)
2 large carrots (sliced)
water
1 packet of vegetable soup mix
2 oz/50 g grated cheddar cheese
1 lb/450 g boiled potato
1-2 tbsp milk

Crumble the minced beef into a saucepan and add the onion, carrots, dried soup mix and sufficient water to cover. Cook for about 30 minutes. When cooked, transfer to an oven proof dish. Mash the potato with the milk and half the cheese and spread on top of the meat mixture. Sprinkle the rest of the cheese over the potato and reheat in the oven. Brown the potato under the grill.

When we arrived in Leeds, we moved into a new house and very shortly, Wendy and Bob Canavan from Dalkeith in Scotland, moved into the house next door. We became good friends over the years and our children, Janet and Adrian, adopted them as 'Auntie Wendy and Uncle Bob'. I remember one incident when we had been away from home over Christmas and returned just after the New Year to a house with 7 or 8 burst pipes and everything completely frozen. Wendy and Bob helped us out with portable heaters and a hot meal. Although Wendy and Bob both come from Dalkeith, near Edinburgh, they have travelled around the country, including living in Northern Ireland and here is Wendy's recipe for cheesecake, which she obtained from a friend in Ireland and which she says is popular with her family. I can also agree it is popular with mine.

WENDY'S EASY-TO-MAKE LEMON CHEESECAKE

Serves 6

10 digestive biscuits (approx 6 oz/175 g) crushed into crumbs
3 oz/80 g butter (or margarine)
1 packet Philadelphia light cream cheese (4 oz/110 g)
$1/2$ cup caster sugar (more or less to taste)
Juice and rind of one lemon
Half lemon jelly
Small tin chilled evaporated milk

Melt the butter/margarine and add crushed biscuits. Press mixture down to form a thinnish base in a flan tin/dish (approximately 8 in/20 cm diameter). Put in the refrigerator to chill. Melt jelly in hot water to make just less than $1/4$ pint/150 ml.

Mix the cream cheese and sugar together, add the lemon juice, rind and the cooled jelly (very runny at this stage). Whip the milk until it is very stiff and then add gradually to the mixture – it will start to thicken and set at his stage. Spread the mixture evenly on top of the biscuit base and chill before serving.

We lived next door to Wendy and Bob for 20 years. Although we often thought of moving house, we were reluctant to move away from such good neighbours. Eventually we moved out to Burley-in-Wharfedale 14 years ago and again have been blessed with good neighbours and here are some of their recipes.

We knew Beryl Caunt when we lived in Adel. She used to help me with Brownies and was known as 'Snowy Owl'. When the house next door to us came on the market, Beryl and Alan bought it and moved in so we were together again. Here are Beryl's recipes for Chocolate and Lime Mousse and Apricot Crunchie.

BERYL'S CHOCOLATE AND LIME MOUSSE

3 oz plain chocolate
2 eggs
1 level tsp sugar
1 lime
5 fluid oz double cream
½ tsp gelatine
Grated chocolate to decorate

Melt the chocolate in a basin over water. Separate the eggs, place yolks in a bowl with sugar and finely grated lime rind. Whisk together, then whisk in melted chocolate. Spoon the lime juice into a small basin and sprinkle over the gelatine. Leave to soak for 10 minutes. Dissolve by standing the bowl in a pan of simmering water until the gelatine clears. Whisk into the chocolate mixture. Beat egg whites and add them to the chocolate mixture, then beat in whipped cream. Decorate with grated chocolate. Cool for 30 minutes before serving.

BERYL'S APRICOT CRUNCHIE

5 oz/150 g margarine
3 oz/80 g Demerera sugar
½ lb/225 g oats
3 oz/80 g golden syrup
3 oz/80 g dried apricots (cut into small pieces)

Cream the margarine and sugar together. Add the syrup, oats and apricots and mix well. Place in a greased Swiss-roll tin. Bake in a moderate oven (180°C/ 350°F/Gas Mark 4) until golden. Mark out the pieces in the tin, but do not remove until they are cool and set.

Sheila and Patrick Quinn are our other 'next door neighbours'. Sheila is an expert flower arranger, teaching this subject for many years. She and I regularly attend the Ilkley Flower Club together. Patrick is a keen ornithologist and has helped us with watching the many bird species which come to our garden. Sheila says *'I rescued this recipe from a rather grubby little recipe book belonging to my mother. I had memories of those moist, tasty slices, spread thickly with butter. Being a domestic science teacher it went into my box of recipe cards and accompanied me from schools to day centres and evening classes, along with its reputation for being simple to make, good to eat and a great keeper. There are two in my freezer at this moment, just in case someone calls or they are needed for a cake stall'.*

SHEILA'S DATE AND WALNUT LOAF

4 oz/110 g plain flour
2 oz/50 g granulated sugar
½ oz/12 g margarine
½ lb/225 g cooking dates
2 oz/50 g walnut pieces
1 level tsp bicarbonate of soda
¼ pint/150 ml boiling water

Grease and line a 1 lb/450 g loaf tin. Chop walnuts finely, cut dates into small pieces and sprinkle over the bicarbonate of soda. Pour boiling water over the dates and stir in well. Leave for 5 minutes.

Sieve flour, rub in margarine and add chopped walnuts and sugar. Stir date mixture into flour mix and pour into well-greased tin and level out. Bake for about 45 minutes until firm at 170°C/335°F/Gas Mark 3. Keep in a tin for 1 – 2 days before eating or freezing.

The author with some of the baby vests, knitted for Maternity Worldwide.

Picture taken from the author's garden in Burley-in-Wharfedale.

Here are other recipes from neighbours and some of their friends. I was pleased to be able to include this next recipe, because on the day we moved into our present house in Burley-in-Wharfedale, David Moodie and his wife Peggy came over with these freshly baked scones. After the trauma of moving, we found then absolutely delicious and such a friendly gesture from our new neighbours.

DAVID AND PEGGY'S FRUIT SCONES

8 oz/225 g SR flour
2 level tsp baking powder
1½ oz/40 g butter
1½ oz/40 g sugar
2 oz/50 g sultanas
1 egg
¼ pint/150 ml milk

Rub in together the flour, baking powder and butter and add in sugar and sultanas. Add the egg and then gradually add the milk to achieve a consistent dough. Roll out the dough to ¾ inch, cut with a scone cutter and place on a greased baking sheet. Bake at 220°C/425°F Gas Mark 7 for 10 minutes.

Katy lives across the road from us and here is her recipe for a Corned Beef Hot dish.

KATY'S CORNED BEEF HOT DISH

Serves 4

One 8 oz/225 g packet of medium egg noodles
1 cup diced corned beef (large tin)
4 oz/110 g cheddar cheese (diced)
1 cup chopped onion (or less to taste)
1 can Cream of Chicken Soup (condensed)
½ can milk

Mix all the ingredients together, put in a casserole and cover with breadcrumbs. Dot with butter and bake at 180°C/350°F Gas Mark 4 for one hour. This is a very tasty dish.

Some of Katy's friends have also contributed recipes which I am very pleased to include.

PAT'S LEMON SOUFFLÉ

Serves 4

³/₄ oz/18 g cornflour
2 large eggs
6 oz/175 g caster sugar
½ pint/275 ml cold milk
2 lemons
¼ oz/6 g gelatine dissolved in 3 tbsp hot water
1 oz/25 g plain chocolate, grated.

Prepare a 5 in/12.5 cm soufflé dish by fitting a band of baking parchment or foil around the outside of the dish to extend to 3 inches above the rim. Blend the cornflour, egg yolks (retain the whites) and half the sugar with a little of the cold milk. Put remaining milk on to heat, adding a few strips of the lemon rind. When milk is almost boiling, pour it onto the blended cornflour, stirring throughout. Remove lemon rind. Return mixture to the pan, bring to the boil, reduce heat and allow to cook for 3 minutes, stirring all the time. Pour mixture into a large bowl, stir in the dissolved gelatine, squeeze the juice from the lemons and stir the juice into the mixture. Leave to cool.

Whisk egg whites until stiff, fold in remaining sugar and fold egg whites into the cooled mixture. Pour into the prepared dish and leave in the refrigerator to set. To serve, carefully remove paper from the dish and decorate the edge of the soufflé with coarsely grated chocolate. If you prefer the lemon flavour to be more intense, simply increase the lemon juice.

MISS S KENDALL'S GINGERBREAD

2 cups self raising flour
1 cup sugar
4 oz/110 g butter or margarine (cut small)
2 tbsp golden syrup
2 tbsp ginger
½ tsp bicarbonate of soda
1 egg
1 cup boiling milk

Put all of the ingredients into a large bowl, add the boiling milk and stir until smooth. Pour into an 8 in/20 cm square tin and cook for approximately 1 hour at 150°C/350°F/ Gas Mark 2. Do not open oven door until cooked. This is a very good recipe, easily made and never fails!

PATRICIA'S MARMALADE CREAM TART

Serves 6

2 or 3 tbsp marmalade
3 eggs
100 g/4 oz sugar
600 ml/1 pint double or whipping cream
Zest of one small orange

For the pastry:
300 g/11 oz plain flour
80 g/3 oz butter
80 g/3 oz lard
Pinch salt
Water to mix pastry, approx ¾ tbsp

Make the pastry and put in a flan dish and bake blind. When cool spread marmalade over the pastry. Whisk together the eggs and sugar, add the cream and orange zest and whisk until it is all blended. Pour into the pastry case and bake for 30-40 minutes at 170°C/335°F/Gas Mark 3. It should still be a little wobbly when cooked. Leave to cool. Sift over with icing sugar and grill to make like brulée.

One of our younger friends, Sam Atkinson, has given me this recipe for curried coleslaw. She likes to make a large quantity and take it to a party.

SAM'S CURRIED COLESLAW

1 white cabbage
4 carrots
2 large onions
Mayonnaise (preferably not the light variety)
1 – 2 tbsp (according to taste) mild curry powder
Two sticks celery (optional)

Grate the carrots and finely chop the onions. Shred the cabbage using a potato peeler to obtain long shreds. Add celery if required. Mix all ingredients in a large bowl, using just 1 tbsp curry powder at first. If desired, add a second tbsp curry powder and mix well. Store in the refrigerator until required. Reduce quantities of ingredients in proportion as required.

Jocelyn Kellett and her husband Ronald have been very good friends for many years. Jocelyn is also an excellent cook and has given me this recipe for Cullen Skink. The name of this rich, tasty soup comes from the fishing village of Cullen, in Morayshire. "Skink" is a soup made originally from a shin of beef. But in this case, the main ingredient is haddock, both smoked and unsmoked.

It is very tasty either hot as part of a meal or cold with oatcakes and biscuits.

JOCELYN'S CULLEN SKINK

Serves 6

1 large onion (Spanish or Egyptian best)
Garlic if desired
2 oz/50 g butter
½ pint/275 ml milk
8 oz/225 g smoked haddock
8 oz/225 g fresh haddock
2 – 3 potatoes, diced into size of large sugar cubes
Salt and pepper
Chopped parsley

Chop onion and simmer in butter (with garlic if desired) in a large pan until softly cooked. Turn into a large bowl and keep warm. In the same pan simmer both the fresh and the smoked haddock in the milk and lift haddock into the bowl when cooked. Boil the potatoes in the same pan until just cooked. Turn into another basin. Using milk from the haddock, make a white sauce and add plenty of cream, pepper and salt and a dash of whisky. Mix all the ingredients together in the bowl – can be any consistency desired from soup to a fish pie. Serve with chopped parsley on top and with oatmeal biscuits, oatcakes or crusty bread.

When we were living in the USA, we met an English couple, David and Maggie Sheen in Providence, Rhode Island. They returned to live in Leeds and, when we first moved to Leeds ourselves, we took a council flat on the 5th floor. The lift was broken and it proved impossible for the removal men to move in our piano and long settee. It was then late in the evening and Maggie and David proved to be true friends and very kindly agreed that these items could be moved into their home and stored in their conservatory. Maggie gave me this recipe for 'sticky bottoms' and says *'I received this recipe from an Estonian friend, Maili, who died from cancer. As a child she escaped across Europe with her mother, brother and sister during the Second World War and spent her teenage years on the West coast of the USA. This recipe probably originates from Estonia'.*

MAGGIE'S STICKY BOTTOMS

Makes about 18 rolls

1 dry yeast envelope or equivalent
½ cup warm water
⅔ cup margarine or butter
½ cup sugar
1 tsp salt
1 cup cooked mashed potato
1 cup scalded milk
2 eggs
6 cups flour (or enough to make a stiff dough)
Raisins
Cinnamon
Melted butter

Put the yeast in the warm water and leave to one side. Combine ingredients as in any dough i.e. scald the milk and add to the margarine, sugar, salt and mashed potato. Beat the eggs and add to the mix, then add the yeast in water. Add the flour and let the mixture rise until it doubles in bulk. Spread rolled-out dough with soft or melted butter, sprinkle generously with sugar and a little cinnamon. Sprinkle generously with raisins and roll up. Cut or slice the roll into 1 inch slices.

In a pan mix 4 tsp melted margarine and ¼ cup of syrup or treacle. Put this in the bottom of a baking tin and loosely pack the slices, cut side down, in the tin. Let rolls double in size. Bake for 20 minutes in a 180°C/350°F/Gas Mark 4 oven, turn tin upside down immediately to remove sticky bottoms. They can be frozen if required.

When Stan first came to work in Leeds, he worked with another biochemist, Dr Jack Salway. Stan, Jack, Nicky (Jack's wife) and myself (and our respective children) became very good friends and have kept in contact, even though Jack and Nicky moved to Surrey in the mid 1970s. Jack has given me this recipe for Thai Lamb Curry. Jack says *'My cousin John's wife, Helen, served this Thai Lamb Curry with a vegetable stir–fry and rice for lunch one Sunday when we were visiting. I can honestly say it was one of the most delicious meals I have ever enjoyed and Helen very kindly copied out the recipe for us. Since then we have served this to numerous dinner party guests who have all been very impressed including the author of this cookery book'.*

JACK'S THAI LAMB CURRY

Serves 4

1 tbsp oil
2 cloves garlic (crushed)
1 onion finely sliced
1 tbsp ground coriander
Half tsp cinnamon
4 green cardamoms, lightly crushed
3 red chillies, deseeded and chopped (or less if preferred)
1 in/2.5 cm piece of fresh root ginger, chopped
350 g/12 oz lean leg of lamb chopped into cubes
1 piece lemon grass
4 lime leaves
275 ml/$\frac{1}{2}$ pint lamb stock
110 g/4 oz creamed coconut

Heat oil and fry garlic and onion until nearly brown. Add coriander, cinnamon, cardamoms, chillies and ginger and stir-fry for 1 minute. Add the lamb and fry until brown. Stir in lemon grass, lime leaves and stock and simmer gently, covered for 50-60 minutes. Five minutes before the end, stir in the creamed coconut. Serve garnished with fresh coriander.

Janet Munroe, a local MacMillan nurse, has been a very good friend to me in recent months and has given me this recipe for Baked Spiced Fish.

JANET'S BAKED SPICED FISH

Serves 4

4 large white fish fillets
3 garlic cloves (peeled and crushed)
Grated zest and juice of one lemon
Grated zest and juice of one lime
2 tbsp chopped fresh coriander
2 tbsp chopped fresh parsley
1 large pinch powdered saffron
1 large pinch tumeric
1 tsp ground cumin
½ tsp ground cinnamon
1 – 2 tsp hot chilli sauce
2 tsp brown sugar

Combine all of the ingredients for the spice mixture in a bowl, adding plenty of salt and pepper and whisk together with a fork. Spoon the spice mixture onto the fish fillets and rub well in, ensuring that each piece is completely coated. Leave to marinate in a cool place for 30 – 60 minutes, no longer or the acid in the marinade will begin to 'cook' the fish. Wrap each filet in a piece of foil and place on a baking sheet. Bake in oven at 200°C/400°F/Gas Mark 6 for 10 – 15 minutes or until fish flakes easily with a fork. Unwrap and transfer to warmed serving plate. Pour liquid from foil onto fish and serve with salad and rice – gorgeous.

In recent years we have attended classes for ballroom dancing and the following recipes were provided by Ivor and Janet Watson, a couple who were part of our dancing class. Janet says *'I like this particular recipe because I love chocolate and cherries and it is a nice 'surprise' to find chocolate at the bottom of the coconut'.*

JANET'S COCONUT SURPRISE

4 oz/110 g sugar
2 oz/50 g butter
4 oz/110 g coconut
2 oz/50 g sultanas
2 oz/50 g glace cherries
1 egg
6–8 oz/175-225 g cake chocolate

Line a Swiss roll tin in foil, melt the chocolate and pour into the tin, leaving to set. Cream the butter and sugar and add the beaten egg. Add coconut, sultanas and cherries. Spread over chocolate. Bake at 180°C/350°F/Gas Mark 4 until golden brown (15 - 20 minutes), leave until cold and cut into pieces.

Ivor says 'This recipe is easy and quick to prepare. If required to be made hot, just add a red chilli. Also, all of the ingredients can be bought at one store'.

IVOR'S CHICKEN CURRY WITH CHIPATIS

Serves 4 - 6

Curry
2 tbsp oil
½ tsp cumin seeds
½ tsp ground cinnamon
2 onions, chopped
1 tsp chopped root ginger
2 cloves garlic
3 chicken breasts cut into slices
14 oz/400 g can tomatoes
1 tbsp soy sauce
2 tsp sugar

Heat the oil, then fry the cumin seeds and cinnamon for 1 minute. Add the onions, ginger and garlic and fry for 2 minutes. Add the chicken and stir fry for 5 minutes until brown. Add the tomatoes and juice, soy sauce and sugar to taste.

Chipati
8 oz/225 g wholemeal flour
1 tsp salt
⅓ pint/180 ml water

Place the flour and salt in a bowl. Stir in water and bind to a soft dough. Knead for 10 minutes, then leave for 30 minutes. Split into 12 pieces and roll out into thin pancakes. Heat a little oil in a frying pan and cook until blisters appear. Turn over until brown. Keep warm in oven and serve warm.

Gordon Hamflett has been a friend for many years since we lived in Adel. Here is his wife Margaret's recipe for fish pie. Margaret says *'My aunt used to make this fish pie as a matter of course, way back in the last century. I started taking the BBC Good Food Magazine last year and also subscribed to it for my sons. Guess what turned up? Fish Pie à la Auntie Edna, circa 1960'.*

MARGARET'S FISH PIE

Serves 4

Smoked undyed haddock for 4 persons (around 1½ lb/675 g)
½ pint/275 ml milk
2 lb 4 oz/1 kg potatoes – King Edward best
6 oz/175 g grated Lancashire cheese
6 /175 g frozen prawns
1 egg

Hard boil the egg and leave to cool. Boil the potatoes retaining the water and mash. Place the fish in a pan with the milk and cook until flaky. Strain the fish and reserve the stock. Flake the fish into a large dish, removing any bones or skin. Chop the egg and layer on top of the fish.

Using the fish stock and some corn flour, make a sauce and make up with the potato water if it becomes too dry (nothing wasted by Aunt Edna). Pour the sauce over the egg and fish and cover with mashed potato.

Grate the cheese and sprinkle on top. Salt and pepper can be used where desired, but the smoked haddock is quite tasty by itself. Place in a hot oven until thoroughly heated and the potato has begun to brown. Serve hot.

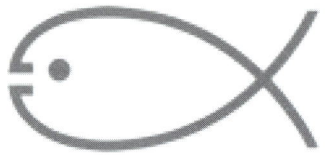

I met Kate Burns when we both attended upholstery classes. Kate has given this Meatloaf recipe which she says she always seemed to be asked to make for end of term parties.

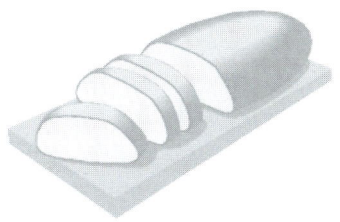

KATE'S MEATLOAF

Serves 6

1lb/450 g beef mince
3 oz/80 g finely chopped mushrooms
2 oz/50 g fresh breadcrumbs
4 oz/110 g streaky bacon
1 clove garlic
1 small onion
1 tsp oregano or thyme
3 tbsp tomato ketchup
1 large egg
Salt and pepper

For the filling
4 oz/110 g blue cheese
1 tbsp top of the milk
1 egg
Pinch cayenne pepper

Mix the bacon, breadcrumbs, mushrooms, onion, egg and garlic in a food processor. Remove and then mix with the other ingredients in a bowl, seasoning well with salt and pepper. Grease and line a 2lb/1 kg loaf tin and heat the oven to 180°C/350°F/Gas Mark 4.

Now make the filling by beating the egg and adding the milk, the cheese and a pinch of cayenne pepper until a smooth consistency is obtained. Spoon half the meat mixture into the tin and spread all the filling mix over it. Cover with the remaining meat mixture. Bake in the centre of the oven for 1 hour. Leave to cool and set then remove from the tin and place on a baking tray.

Turn up the oven to 240°C/465°F/Gas Mark 9. Smear with 3 tbsp of tomato ketchup. Bake for 15 minutes.

For many years while our children were younger we were lucky enough to have a permanently rented farm cottage in Northumberland. We would often go there for long weekends and for longer periods in the holidays. It was a small, but close-knit community and one of our neighbours was Eileen Scott whose children played for long hours with Janet and Adrian. Next door lived the local blacksmith and two doors from us lived Mr Charles Ophield. After we gave up the cottage in the mid-nineties, we continued to keep in touch with Charles and were fortunate enough to have him visit us in Yorkshire a few years ago, soon after his one hundredth birthday. Eileen Scott is now a physiotherapist, living in the Scottish borders, but we also keep in touch with her and she has contributed this recipe for Sticky Toffee Pudding.

EILEEN'S STICKY TOFFEE PUDDING

Serves 6 - 8

Pudding
6 oz/175g dates (chopped)
½ pint/275 ml boiling water
1 tsp vanilla essence
1 tsp bicarbonate of soda
6 oz/175 g margarine (or butter)
6 oz/175 g caster sugar
1 egg (whisked)
8 oz/225g plain flour
1 tsp baking powder

Toffee
5 oz/150g dark brown sugar
3 oz/80 g butter
4 tbsp double cream

Place the dates, vanilla essence, bicarbonate of soda and boiling water in a bowl and leave to cool. Meanwhile blend the margarine and sugar until light and fluffy. Add the whisked egg. Sieve together the flour and baking powder and stir into the creamed mixture. Gradually add the cooled liquid ingredients.

Place the mixture into a greased loaf tin and bake in a moderately hot oven (180°C/350°F/Gas Mark 4) for approximately 45 minutes.

Make the toffee by placing all the ingredients in a saucepan and boil for 5 minutes. When the pudding is cooked, pour the toffee over and place under a hot grill until the toffee bubbles, taking care not to burn the toffee. Alternatively, serve up the pudding individually and pour the toffee over. Serve with pouring cream or as an alternative try custard or ice-cream.

This is a good pudding to freeze. Enjoy it many times.

CHAPTER 5

SHETLAND

MY FATHER was from the Shetland Islands, or Shetland, as it is more usually known. It is the most northerly part of the British Isles, further north than Orkney and a long 12 – 14 hour ferry trip from Aberdeen. Shetland lies at latitude 60 degrees north, the same latitude as the southern tip of Greenland. It is nearer to Bergen in Norway than to Aberdeen and nearer to the Arctic Circle than to London. Shetland was invaded by the Norsemen in the late 8th and early 9th centuries and has a strong Viking tradition. It was given to Scotland by King Christian I of Denmark and Norway as a dowry for his daughter's marriage to the future King James III of Scotland.

Shetland has almost 1000 miles of spectacular coastline, with fantastic cliff scenery, many 'voes' (rather like Norwegian fjords) and beautiful beaches. In mid-summer, it never gets dark, when the light is described as the 'Simmer Dim'.

When I was a child, we would sometimes visit my grandparents in Lerwick (Shetlands's capital) for summer holidays. I enjoyed fishing for pilticks (saithe) in the harbour. Lerwick was a very busy herring port in those days and it was incredible to watch the women cleaning the herring at such a speed, barrel after barrel full. Sadly the herring were over-fished and few signs of the herring industry can be seen today. However, the herring numbers are picking up and I hope we won't be foolish enough to fish them out again. There is a lot to be said for a fresh baked herring. Here is my recipe:

ANNE'S BAKED HERRING

Serves 4

8 herrings (filleted and cleaned)
1 medium onion chopped
Salt, pepper and malt vinegar.
A little flour for dusting.

Wash and dry the herring on kitchen roll. Season with a little salt and pepper, then spread some chopped onion over the fish and sprinkle with a little malt vinegar. Roll each fish carefully from top to tail and secure with a cocktail stick. Dust the outer side with flour to give an attractive finish. Place fish on a baking tray and bake in a moderately hot oven (180°C/350°F/Gas Mark 4), for about 30 minutes.

Allow fish to cool thoroughly and serve with salad and crusty bread.

The fishing industry is still very important to the Shetland economy. Nowadays it is white fish (haddock, cod, and whiting) or mackerel. Many Shetlanders have boats and go after a few fish themselves. There is nothing tastier than a freshly caught mackerel fried on board before returning home after a successful fishing trip.

In recent years Shetland has become active in fish farming and became well known for its farmed salmon. However, over production resulted in low prices as well as disease and, whereas just a few years ago almost every voe seemed to be taken over by salmon cages, now this industry is less obvious and healthier methods of farming are being pursued. My cousin Julia gave me this recipe for oven-baked salmon.

JULIA'S BAKED STUFFED SALMON

Serves 6 (depending on size of fish)

1 salmon (preferably wild)
1 onion
2 carrots
1 cup breadcrumbs
4 oz/110 g butter
1 tsp salt
1 egg

Grate the onion and carrots and cook gently in melted butter for five minutes. Add breadcrumbs and stir until they begin to brown. Remove from heat and allow to cool. Mix in the egg and salt.

Make sure the fish is thoroughly cleaned, with scales, gills and entrails removed. Wipe the inside and fill with stuffing.

Place the fish in a well-greased baking dish, dust with flour and place a few dots of butter on top. Bake in a moderately hot oven for 30 minutes. Serve hot with lemon wedges and parsley, or cold with mayonnaise.

Note: If you have the patience, remove as many bones as possible (safer to eat and makes more room for extra stuffing).

One summer when Jean and I were staying with Grandma she went to the farmer's market and bought a caddy lamb (a lamb that needs to be bottle fed). Jean and I enjoyed playing with the lamb on the back lawn and feeding it with a bottle. Imagine our horror when, at Christmas time, a parcel arrived at our home containing a leg of our very own lamb.

Shetland is well-known for its hospitality and this is well-illustrated by an experience many years ago, when Stan first visited Shetland with me. We decided to visit Burra Isle which, in those days, was only connected to the Mainland of Shetland by a little ferry service to Scalloway, Shetland's ancient capital. In more recent years, a bridge has been built. We took the ferry from Scalloway to Burra and on the way across, we met a sea-going captain returning to his home in Burra Isle after a spell at sea. He invited us to his house for tea. The house was high on the hillside with a lovely view out over the other islands and there we had tea and 'Bronnie Cake'. Afterwards, Stan and I toured the island but, unfortunately, we walked too far and as we rounded the headland back to the harbour, we could see the last ferry of the day, having just left for Scalloway. We were really downcast as we didn't know what to do. Just then, two of the locals came over on a motorbike and said they had a small motorboat and would take us back to Scalloway. So we had a very pleasant trip back, they wouldn't take any payment and all was well thanks to the kindness of the people of Burra. That's what it was like in Shetland in those days and I have no doubt that, if no boat had been available, one of the locals would have looked after us for the night. The recipe for Bronnie Cake has been given by Rowena Wiseman.

Well camouflaged seals basking on the rocks. The camouflage may be to hide them from their only natural predator in Shetland, the killer whale.

Gannets nest in large cliff-based colonies in Shetland and may be seen diving spectacularly for food, mainly sand eels.

ROWENA'S SHETLAND BRONNIE CAKE

2 cups SR flour
1 tsp baking powder
1/4 tsp salt
1/2 cup sugar
3/4 cup raisins
1 egg
3 oz/80 g margarine
Milk to mix

Sieve the dry ingredients into a basin and rub in the margarine. Add the raisins, egg and enough milk to mix to a soft consistency. Bake in a hot oven (220°C/425°F/Gas Mark 7) for 3/4 hour. When cooled, slice and serve buttered.

My aunt Annie comes from Fetlar which is an island off the east side of the Shetland mainland and is known as the 'Garden of Shetland'. Fetlar hit the national news in the 1980s when a pair of snowy owls was found to be breeding there, a first for the UK. They returned to breed each year for quite a few years, but have not been seen for some time now. Recently, I found this recipe for Clapshott (a mixture of swede and potato) in one of Annie's Fetlar recipe books. Essentially, it is the same dish as is now served in some of the 'posh' restaurants, but I'm sure they don't put it on the menu as Clapshott. Here is the recipe.

SHETLAND CLAPSHOTT

Turnips (or swede)
Potatoes
Knob of butter
Salt and pepper

Use 1 part turnips to two parts potatoes. Boil sliced turnips for about 15 minutes and then add the potatoes, peeled and whole. Boil for a further 20 minutes. Drain off the water and then season to taste with salt and pepper. Add a good sized knob of butter and mash together thoroughly. Serve piping hot.

Annie often makes excellent cheese scones and here is her recipe, along with one from her friend Adeline, whose favourite is John Bull Slab.

ANNIE'S CHEESE SCONES

4 oz/110 g self raising flour
4 oz/110 g grated cheese
1 oz/25 g caster sugar
1 egg
¼ pint/150 ml milk
2 oz/50 g margarine
3 oz/80 g raisins (optional)

Preheat oven to 230°C/450°F/Gas Mark 8.
   Sift the flour and baking powder. Add the sugar and raisins (optional). Rub in the margarine. Mix to a soft dough with beaten egg and milk. Turn on to a lightly floured board and knead quickly. Cut into circles with a scone cutter and place on a greased baking tray. Bake for 15 minutes.

ADELINE'S JOHN BULL SLAB

3 tbsp sugar
3 tbsp rolled oats
3 tbsp SR flour
3 tbsp coconut
3 tbsp butter
½ tbsp golden syrup

Preheat oven to 160°C/325°F/Gas Mark 3. Thoroughly mix all ingredients except the butter. Melt the butter and pour over the other ingredients. Press into a roasting tin and bake for about 25 minutes.

One of our friends in Shetland, Roy Patterson, has a small boat and regularly goes out among the islands setting his crab and lobster creels. He is very generous with his catch and we are sometimes lucky enough to get a sample of his dressed crab or lobster.   He has contributed a recipe for a seafood omelette. Roy says *'this dish was created for the writer Arnold Bennett (1867–1931) by the chef at the Savoy Grill. It is simple to make and makes a superb "stand alone" meal'.*

ROY'S OMELETTE ARNOLD BENNETT

Serves 4

1-2 fillets of smoked haddock
4 eggs
2 oz/50 g butter
1 oz/25 g SR flour
½ pint/175 ml milk
2-3 oz/50-80 g grated cheese
Black pepper
1 tbsp double cream

Poach the fillet of smoked haddock in the milk with a knob of butter and a little pepper. Strain off the milk after poaching and use it to make a cheese sauce with the flour, 2 oz/50 g of grated cheese and 1 oz/25 g of butter. Beat the eggs with the double cream and add the cooked fillet (broken into small chunks).

Melt a knob of butter in a frying pan over a low heat, add the egg and fish mixture and cook until set as an omelette. Pour some hot cheese sauce over the omelette, scatter the remaining grated cheese on top and place the pan under a hot grill until the omelette is browned on the top. Serve immediately.

Everyone's favourites, Shetland ponies.

Another recipe containing smoked haddock was given to me by Elizabeth Garrick. She used to live in an old croft house called 'The Skoes' in Sandsound on the West of Shetland. The Skoes has a beautiful position overlooking Sandsound Voe and beach and the distant islands and seals and otters are often to be seen. When she and her husband moved to a new bungalow about a mile away, we became the new owners of The Skoes and our family and friends have had many happy times there.

ELIZABETH'S BAKED SMOKED HADDOCK

Serves 3 - 4

1 lb/450 g smoked haddock fillets
Milk
1 large egg

Cut the fillets into large chunks and place in a casserole dish. Cover with milk and cook in a moderate oven for about 30 minutes.
Lightly beat 1 large egg and pour it over the fish and milk. Continue cooking until the egg has set around the fish.
Serve with mashed potatoes and peas. This is a good recipe for cooking in a Rayburn or similar.

At the end of the 1970s, oil was discovered in the North Sea around Shetland. Over 5,000 oil and construction workers arrived to build the largest oil terminal in Europe, with both advantages and disadvantages for the community. The North Sea oil from the British sector is piped to Sullom Voe in Shetland and into huge tanks, from where it is transferred into tankers and taken to every part of the world. Nowadays, although North Sea oil still comes ashore in Shetland and further finds are now arriving from the deeper Atlantic Ocean, unless you knew where to look, you would never suspect that so much oil is being landed in Shetland.

The next recipe is for Sweet and Sour Chicken and was given to me by Rowena Wiseman.

ROWENA'S SWEET AND SOUR CHICKEN

Serves 4

1lb /450 g chicken breasts (skinned)
2 onions (sliced)
2 level tbsp brown sugar
3 level tbsp tomato paste
1 level tbsp corn flour
3 tbsp vinegar
2 tbsp soy sauce
1 red pepper (sliced)
$3/4$ pint/425 ml stock
Salt and pepper

Cut the chicken into cubes and brown in oil. Remove from the pan. Add the onions and red pepper to the pan and fry gently for 2 minutes. Remove the pan from the heat and stir in sugar, tomato paste, vinegar and soy sauce. Blend corn flour with a little stock, then add the rest of the stock. Pour into the pan and bring to the boil, stirring. Add the chicken and seasoning and simmer for about 30 minutes.

Serve with rice or pasta plus a green vegetable. Chicken can be replaced by pork or if a vegetarian dish is required, by vegetables.

Rowena's husband, Johnny, is a baker and has given this recipe for Shetland Bannocks, one of the most typical of Shetland foods.

JOHNNY'S SHETLAND BANNOCKS

2 lb/900 g soft plain flour
4 oz/110 g fat (e.g. Cookeen)
$1^{1}/_{2}$ oz/35 g baking powder
$1/4$ oz/6 g salt
$1^{1}/_{4}$ pints/720 ml milk.

Sieve the dry ingredients into a basin. Rub in the fat and add enough milk to mix to a stiff dough. Knead well on a floured board. Divide the mixture into 6 balls and roll out to approximately $3/8$ inch/1 cm thick. Cut each round into four.

Heat griddle to moderate heat and bake bannocks for approximately 2 minutes on each side. This makes 24 Shetland Bannocks.

'The Skoes' and Sandsound Voe, Shetland.

'Muckle Flugga', the most northerly point in the British Isles – no more land in this direction before the North Pole.

Finally, in this section, I include a mixed collection of favourite recipes from my many aunts and cousins in Shetland.

HAZEL'S COD BAKE

Serves 4

1½ lb/680 g fresh spinach (or 10 oz/275 g frozen chopped spinach, cooked as package instructions)
4 cod steaks (or any other firm fish)
2 oz/ 50 g butter
¼ tsp ground nutmeg
Salt and freshly ground black pepper
Cheese Sauce
1 oz/25 g butter
1 oz/25 g flour
¾ pint/425 ml milk
4 oz/110 g grated cheddar cheese

Wash the fresh spinach and place in a large saucepan with salt to taste. Cook gently until tender. Drain well and chop finely. Season the cooked spinach with plenty of black pepper and the nutmeg. Stir in half the butter. Place in a shallow ovenproof dish.

Fry fish in the remaining butter for 2-3 minutes each side. Place fish on top of the spinach.

Make the cheese sauce using half the cheese. Melt the butter in a small saucepan. Remove it from heat and stir in the flour. Add the milk, stirring as you add it. Bring to the boil then add half the cheese and stir until melted into the sauce. Pour the sauce over the fish and sprinkle with the remaining cheese. Bake for 20-30 minutes in the oven (190°C/375°F/Gas Mark 5). Serve immediately.

BETH'S OATCAKES

4 cups fine oatmeal
1 cup plain flour
2 level tsp salt
1 tsp baking soda
8 oz/225 g butter (or half margarine/half butter)
Good half cup water

Mix the oatmeal, flour and salt. Melt the butter/margarine to boiling point and add to oatmeal with the water. Mix thoroughly, flatten with a rolling pin to quite a thin layer and cut into squares. Bake in an oven at 230°C/450°F/Gas Mark 8 and check after 10 minutes.

LOUISE'S SPECIAL SOUP

Serves 6

4-5 carrots (peeled and chopped)
2 medium onions (peeled and chopped)
2 rashers of bacon (cut into pieces and grilled or fried)
1 cup of lentils
2 chicken stock cubes
1-2 cloves of garlic (chopped)
Water
Salt and pepper
Vegetable oil

Pour a little oil into a large saucepan. Fry the chopped onions and garlic gently in the oil, but do not allow them to brown. Remove the pan from the heat and add the carrots and bacon. Wash the lentils in a sieve and add to the pan. Dissolve the stock cubes in 2 pints/1,140 ml of boiling water and add to the pan. Season with salt and pepper. Simmer the soup gently for about 1 hour adding more water if needed. Serve with crusty bread.

AUNTIE BABA'S SCOTTISH PANCAKES (DROP SCONES)

8 oz/225 g SR flour
2 level tsp baking powder
2 tbsp sugar
2 tbsp syrup
2 eggs
Milk to mix

Sieve the flour, sugar and baking powder. Make a hole in the centre and drop the eggs and syrup and milk into the well. Whisk everything together until a creamy consistency. Stand for 10 minutes with a dish towel on top.

Heat the griddle with the margarine, drop in a spoonful of mix until bubbles form. Turn onto other side. When cooked, place on a plate and cover with a dish towel. Pour on sugar as required.

AUNTIE LIZZIE'S GINGERBREAD

2 cups plain flour
1 tsp ground ginger
1 tsp mixed spice
1 tsp baking soda
1 cup fruit
1 cup soft brown sugar
¼ cup margarine/butter
1 tbsp black treacle
1 cup cold water
2 tsp finely chopped walnuts
1 egg – well beaten

Simmer the fruit, sugar, margarine/butter, treacle and cold water for 5 minutes. Allow to cool, add the egg and spoon in the sieved dry ingredients. Mix well. Line and grease a 7" cake tin and cook at 180°C/350°F/Gas Mark 4 for 1½ hours.

HAZEL'S QUICK BROWN BREAD

8 oz/225 g wholemeal flour
8 oz/225 g plain flour
1 tsp salt
1 tsp bicarbonate of soda
1 tsp cream of tartar
¼ pint/150 ml warm milk
½ pint/275 ml warm water
1 tbsp honey
1 tsp balsamic vinegar

Set the oven to 200°C/400°F/Gas Mark 6. Grease a 2 lb/900 g loaf tin. Put the wholemeal flour in a warm bowl and sift into the bowl the plain flour, salt, bicarbonate of soda and cream of tartar. Add vinegar and honey to the warm milk and water and stir. Pour this into the dry ingredients, stir quickly and mix thoroughly with a spoon. (At this stage, up to 2 oz/50 g roughly chopped walnuts can be added (if desired). Bake at 200°C/400°F/Gas Mark 6 for 20 minutes, then at 180°C/350°F/Gas Mark 4 for 30 minutes. Turn onto a wire rack until cool.

BUNTY'S SPONGE CAKE

5 oz/150 g SR flour
¼ level tsp baking powder
½ level tsp salt
3 oz/80 g margarine
4 oz/110 g caster sugar
2 eggs
2½ tbsp milk
Few drops vanilla essence

Lightly grease two 7 inch/25 cm sandwich tins and line the bottom of the tins. Sift the flour, baking powder and salt together. Cream the margarine and add the sugar until light and fluffy. Beat the eggs in one at a time. Lightly fold in the sifted ingredients alternately with the milk and vanilla essence. Turn into prepared tins and bake in a moderate oven 180°C/350°F/Gas Mark 4 for approximately 20-25 minutes (less for a fan-assisted oven).

Fillings
2 oz/50 g margarine
5 oz/150 g icing sugar
1 tbsp evaporated milk

Cream the margarine and blend in the sifted icing sugar alternately with the milk. For a chocolate cream, sift in 3 level tbsp Cocoa with the icing sugar and add an extra ½ tbsp evaporated milk. For a coffee cream, blend in 1 tbsp powdered coffee with the evaporated milk, before mixing with the other ingredients.

BUNTY'S FAVOURITE MACARONI CHEESE

Serves 4

3 cups shortcut macaroni per person
2 medium onions, chopped
1 tbsp olive oil
5 oz/150 g strong Cheddar cheese (grated)
1 8 oz/230 g tin chopped tomatoes with herbs
2 rounded tsp plain flour
1 cup milk
Salt, pepper and garlic granules
Tomato for decoration

Place the macaroni in a large pan and cover with cold water, season, bring to the boil and cook according to the packet instructions. Stir frequently, adding more boiled water as necessary. When soft, rinse with boiled water and drain.

To make the sauce, cook the chopped onions in the oil until soft. Mix the flour with the milk and add to the onions, simmer for approximately 2 minutes, stirring constantly. Add the tin of tomatoes and 4 oz/110 g cheese with the salt, pepper and garlic granules to taste. Bring back to the boil and then simmer for a further 2 minutes.

Place the sauce in a large oven-proof dish and stir in the drained macaroni. Sprinkle the remaining cheese on top and decorate with slices of tomato. Place under a heated grill to brown.

Serve immediately with a green salad and enjoy.

CHAPTER 6
WALKERS' GROUP

THE 'Ladies Walkers' Group' was originally formed by a number of ladies who knew each other and who lived in Adel, Leeds. Gradually, other members like myself joined the Group, as well as others from outside the area. We meet alternate Mondays throughout the year and take it in turn to plan and lead a walk. This mainly involves a preliminary reconnoitre the previous weekend with a partner, to check the route and look out for difficulties such as broken stiles, bulls in fields and other hazards.

The walks tend to centre around a couple of hours in the morning, then a pub lunch or sandwiches, followed by the second part of the walk – total distance around 8 miles. I occasionally lead a walk, but have to admit that it is usually without adequate planning. Mostly I get away with it, but sometimes this runs into problems.

The walks are especially good because we are fortunate enough to live in the beautiful Yorkshire Dales, where the scenery and views are quite spectacular. There are literally hundreds of public footpaths within our walking range and we really are spoiled for choice. Besides the good physical exercise, the walks are a great opportunity to chat and to get to know people well. There is also a corresponding 'Mens Walking Group' and we have joint walks on some occasions. Most of the ladies in our Walking Group have kindly supplied recipes for the book and these are included below.

Margaret Peacock, one of my walking friends, was given the following recipe for parkin over 30 years ago by a relation of 'Aunt Mildred'. She has made large amounts over the years and it is a substantial addition to a walker's lunch pack. Margaret says, 'Mildred Hallam lived in the small village of Dungworth, which lies 7 miles northwest of Sheffield. Mildred was born in Dungworth in 1901 and grew up on a farm where she learned the skills of cooking from an early age. Her mother had been making this parkin from about 1880, when she married. Mildred too married a farmer and moved to Padley Farm, in the same village, where she continued to produce home cooked food. Her daughter Betty still bakes this parkin recipe and so do several friends and relations. The parkin will keep very well in an airtight tin or will freeze. Parkin is traditionally kept in a tin with a sliced Cox's apple to keep it damp (not compulsory) and left to mature for at least a week and, as Yorkshire cooks will tell you, allow it to 'come again'. However, in our house, it is eaten straight away'.

Brenda Short says "I'm a real slow cooker fan because I like to have a good hot meal ready to return to after a day out walking and with a slow cooker it is never overdone. You can also use cheaper cuts of meat because of the long gentle cooking'.

AUNT MILDRED'S PARKIN

8 oz/225 g butter or margarine
8 oz/225 g golden syrup
8 oz/225 g self raising flour
8 oz/225 g fine oatmeal
8 oz/225 g dark muscovado sugar
2 tsp ground ginger
1 egg, beaten and made up with 1/3 pint/180 ml milk
1/2 tsp baking powder.

Preheat oven to 160°C/325°F/Gas Mark 3. Thoroughly grease a 10 inch/25 cm square cake tin. Melt the butter and golden syrup together in a saucepan (do not allow to boil). Mix all the dry ingredients together in a mixing bowl and stir in the melted ingredients. Add the egg and the milk and thoroughly combine using a wooden spoon. Pour into the well-greased tin and bake in the oven for approximately 45 minutes. Remove from the tin whilst still warm to avoid sticking.

BRENDA'S BEEF GOULASH

Serves 8

2 1/4 lb/1 kg stewing steak (cut up)
3 tbsp flour
Salt and pepper
3 tbsp oil
3 onions chopped
2 green peppers sliced
1/2 pint/275 ml beef stock
14 oz/400 g can of tomatoes
3 tbsp tomato puree
1 tbsp paprika
1 sachet of Bouquet Garni
A little soured cream or yoghurt to garnish

Pre-heat slow cooker on high. Season the flour and toss the pieces of meat in it. Heat the oil in a large frying pan add the meat and cook until browned. Stir in the onion and peppers and cook for 3 minutes. Stir in the remaining ingredients and bring to the boil. Transfer to the slow cooker. Cook on low for 7-10 hours. Discard the Bouquet Garni, adjust the seasoning and serve with a swirl of soured cream or yoghurt.
Alternatively the goulash can be cooked in a casserole dish in the oven.

A Typical winter's scene near Ilkley in the Yorkshire Dales.

Another of my walking friends, Cath Potts, lived in the USA for some time. She says, 'This recipe was given to me by Helga, a great friend who I met in the USA in 1971 when we were moving into our apartment in Gaithersburg, Maryland. She invited us round for a light lunch. In no time at all we were all enjoying this recipe served with bread and a green salad, accompanied by her own contribution, Sangria. What a welcome into a new area!'.

KATH'S EXOTIC CHICKEN SALAD

Serves 10

6-10 cooked chicken breasts, diced and seasoned to taste.
2 cans water chestnuts
2 lb seedless grapes, halved
2-3 cups almonds, roasted and chopped
2 cups of celery, chopped
2 cups mayonnaise
1 tbs curry powder
2 tbs lemon juice

Mix the first 5 ingredients together
Mix the last 3 ingredients together to make a flavoured dressing
Add the dressing to the chicken salad.

Here are some more recipes which are for sandwiches or snacks to take when out walking, or for some simple meals to come home to. The next recipe comes from Fiji and is originally a recipe for cooking turtle. The meat is cooked in its own juices by steaming or in an earthen oven. Kovu is the method of cooking. In Fiji this would be served with dalo or cassava and rourou. Dalo and cassava are root vegetables and rourou is a green vegetable like spinach. They can be bought in Indian shops and markets.

HILARY'S LAMB KOVU

Serves 6 - 8

2 lb/900 g diced lamb
2 onions
2 tomatoes
Chilli to taste (1-2 Bird's Eye chillies cut in rings so they are recognisable)
Salt and pepper
Banana leaves or foil
(Since banana leaves are difficult to obtain, a double layer of foil can be used - as advised by Adi Mei Rabukowonga, wife of a past High Commissioner)

Place a double layer of foil in a casserole dish and fill with a mixture of diced lamb, chopped onion, chopped tomato, salt, pepper ad finely chopped chilli. There is no need for any liquid, as the natural juices suffice. Seal both sheets of foil well and cook in the oven at 180°C/350°F/Gas Mark 4 for 2-2½ hours. Serve with boiled potatoes and green vegetables.

LIZ'S LEMON CRUNCH

16 digestive biscuits (crumbled)
4 oz/110 g butter or margarine
14 oz/397 g can of condensed milk
½ pint/275 ml double cream
2 lemons, finely grated and squeezed

Melt the butter in a pan and add the biscuit crumbs. Mould into a 7 inch/25 cm flan dish, covering base and sides. (If the lemon crunch is to be frozen, line the dish first with foil). Mix together the condensed milk, cream and lemon rind in a basin. Add most of the lemon juice and stir. Leave mixture to thicken for a few minutes. Add more juice after 5 minutes if not set enough. Pour into the flan dish and refrigerate.

MARGARET'S MIXED FISH PATÉ

Serves 12

7½ oz/200 g can red salmon
7½ oz/200 g can tuna in oil
4 oz/110 g prawns or shrimps
1 can anchovies pureed or 2 tbsp anchovy essence (optional)
4 oz/110 g melted butter
½ pint/275 ml single cream
6 oz/175 g breadcrumbs
Juice and rind of 1 lemon
Salt and pepper

Remove the bone and dark skin from the salmon. Flake the fish and chop the prawns. Mix the breadcrumbs, lemon juice and grated rind, butter and cream in a bowl. Add all the fish and anchovy essence, if using and gently stir. Put into 12 ramekin dishes or 1 large bread tin. Chill in fridge. This also freezes very well.

Enthusiastic Ethiopian children greet Maternity Worldwide staff.

BRENDA'S MOCK CRAB SANDWICHES

Makes 6 sandwiches

Mock crab
¼ lb/110 g tomatoes
3 oz/80 g cheese
1 egg

Scald the tomatoes and pulp. Grate the cheese and add the beaten egg and cheese to the tomatoes. Season with pepper and salt as required. Add a knob of butter and cook the mixture until the cheese has melted. Use the mixture to make tasty moist sandwiches, ideal for a packed lunch.

CHAPTER 7
WORK

SINCE leaving school at 16, I have had many jobs over the years, studying the hard way (part-time whilst working), before obtaining my research-based higher degree at Leeds in 1986.

For 15 years, I enjoyed a teaching career, including 12 years teaching chemistry alongside my colleague Marguerite Mason, who was head of Chemistry. I enclose two of her recipes. For the first, Marguerite says, *'This recipe is especially good for entertaining, because its flavours improve with keeping a day or two and even freezing for a short time. It can then be carefully reheated when needed'.*

MARGUERITE'S SWISS BEEF

Serves 4

3 tbsp oil
3 large onions (sliced)
2 sticks celery (sliced)
1½ lb/675 g blade or chuck steak, in four pieces
2 tbsp plain flour
One 14 oz/400 g can tomatoes
1 tbsp tomato purée
1 clove of garlic (crushed)
Chopped, fresh basil

Heat the oil in a pan. Add the onions and celery and fry gently until just coloured. Transfer to an ovenproof casserole. Sprinkle the steaks with salt and pepper and coat with flour. Add to the pan and brown on both sides and then transfer to the casserole with the vegetables. Sprinkle any leftover flour into the pan and blend into the fat.

Cook, stirring, for one minute and then add the remaining ingredients except the basil. Bring to the boil and pour over the beef. Cover and cook in a pre-heated, moderate oven, (170°C/335°F/Gas Mark 3) for 1½ to 2 hours. Garnish with the basil before serving.

For Marguerite's next recipe, she says, *'This recipe comes from my sister-in-law and we have used it in our family for many years as a change from the usual mince pies at Christmas, or occasionally at other times of year. If you like making meringues, sorbets or other items using only the whites of eggs, this is a convenient way of using the spare yolks'.*

MARGUERITE'S DUKE OF CAMBRIDGE TART

3 oz/80 g margarine
3 oz/80 g sugar
2 egg yolks
2 tbsp rum
4 oz/110 g sultanas or raisins (or a mixture of both)
2 oz/50 g glacé cherries
6 oz/175 g short pastry

Bake an 8 inch/20 cm flan case using the short pastry. Put the dried fruit in a pan, cover with cold water, bring to the boil and cook for 5 minutes. Drain, add the rum and allow to stand overnight.

Melt the sugar and margarine together, remove from the heat and beat in the egg yolks. Add the fruit and the cherries. Fill the flan case with the mixture and bake in an oven at 190°C/375°F/Gas Mark 5 for 30 minutes or until set. Do not overcook as the mixture then dries out. This recipe freezes well.

Whilst teaching, I became friendly with Stella Murdoch, who had the parallel biology class to me and I started helping her with the Young Ornithologist's Club at its weekly meetings. Stella and I took the Club on many interesting outings to local birdwatching sites. I enclose Stella's recipe for 'Lemon Dainty'.

STELLA'S LEMON DAINTY

5 oz/150 g sugar
1 tbsp plain flour
Grated rind of large lemon
1 oz/25 g butter
Yolk of two eggs (beaten)
Whites of two eggs (whipped separately)
1 cup milk

Mix egg yolks, butter and sugar together. Add flour and milk and stir in beaten egg white. Pour into a greased dish and bake at (160°C/300°F/Gas Mark 2-3) for 30 minutes until brown and risen. Serve hot or cold (has a spongy top and a 'gooey' bottom).

One day at school, I had the idea that a pond in the school grounds might be good for attracting birds and the Headmistress gave her consent, provided I did not have to ask the school gardener to dig it out. As the annual school fete was coming up in a few weeks time, I arranged a competition among the fathers of the pupils, where they had to dig out as much soil as possible from a marked out area in a fixed time. The father with the greatest weight of soil was the winner. The marked-out area just 'happened' to be pond-shaped and the event proved both popular and successful, as we ended up with a slightly larger hole than we needed.

After New Year, our school always had an extra week's holiday and five or six of us would gather at the home of Jackie Wilkinson for a delicious lunch and relaxing afternoon. Jackie is an excellent cook and here is her recipe for Chocolate Trifle.

JACKIE'S CHOCOLATE TRIFLE

1 Sponge cake or "flan sponge"
Brandy or Tia Maria
4 eggs
1 pint milk
200g/7 oz bar chocolate (milk or dark, not cooking chocolate) melted with a little milk
One chocolate "Flake"
Whipped cream

Place a layer of sponge soaked in the brandy or Tia Maria in the bottom of a glass trifle bowl. Prepare the egg custard by whisking four eggs with 1 pint/570 ml milk and heating in a microwave oven until of a thick pouring consistency. If the eggs and milk separate, whisk again. Pour half of the custard over the sponge and allow to settle. Follow this with a layer of melted chocolate. Repeat the three layers, sponge, custard and chocolate. Refrigerate until you are ready to serve. Decorate with whipped cream and crumpled chocolate flake.

After retiring from teaching, I returned to work part-time in the research laboratories of the University of Leeds, where I had also worked many years earlier. I very much enjoyed working among the young research students and postdoctoral fellows and many of them provided recipes for me, included below.

AMANDA'S MUSHROOM STROGANOFF

Serves 4 – 6

2 medium onions (sliced)
5 sticks celery (chopped)
50 g/2 oz butter or margarine
450 g/1 lb button mushrooms
½ tsp mixed herbs
½ tsp basil
1 large heaped tbsp unbleached flour
280 ml/1½ pint vegetable stock
65 ml/2½ fl oz soured cream / yoghurt
Salt and pepper
Chopped parsley

Sauté the onions and celery with the butter or margarine over a low heat, in a large pan. Cook until onions are transparent. Add mushrooms and cook for 2 – 3 minutes. Add mixed herbs and basil.

Stir in the flour and cook for 1 minute. Add stock and seasoning and allow to cook gently for 8 – 10 minutes. Remove from the heat and stir in the soured cream. Heat very gently to serving temperature, but do not allow to boil.

Garnish with chopped parsley and serve at once, ideally with wild rice.

David Vernon has given a Scottish recipe. He says *'It was very common in the past in Scotland, to mix whisky with honey and equally common to mix liquid with oatmeal. Bringing the two together is credited to a Duke of Atholl during a Highland rebellion in 1475. He is said to have foiled his enemies by filling the well which they normally drank from with this potent ambrosial mixture, which so intoxicated them that they were easily taken. Some traditional recipes leave the oatmeal in whilst others use only the strained liquid from steeping the oatmeal in water. It may be drunk as a liqueur and is often served on festive occasions such as New Year. Alternatively it may be mixed with a stiffly whipped cream and served with shortbread as a sweet'*

DAVID'S ATHOLL BROSE (AETHELBROSE)

Makes 2-3 litres/3½-5 pints
2-3 cups rolled oats
4½ cups water
4 cups whisky (the better the quality, the better the final result)
1 cup honey
1 cup cream

In a large bowl, mix oats and 3 cups of water, stir and let the mixture sit overnight until the water is totally absorbed. Add 1½ more cups water to the mixture and let it sit for a further 2 hours.

Strain the oat/water mixture through 2 – 3 layers of cheesecloth into a large bowl by squeezing and wringing globs of oatmeal through the cloth, until the oats are nearly free of water. This is messy and requires a lot of effort.
Add whisky, honey and cream to the oat-water. Mix until all ingredients are blended. Best served cold.

Doreen Berger has provided this recipe for salmon cutlets. She says, '*This was a firm favourite at home when I was little. My mother made them using red salmon only, but as I am a 'tuna' person, I improvised with pink salmon and tuna. So experiment and see which combination you prefer!*'

DOREEN'S SALMON CUTLETS

Makes 20 cutlets

400 g/14 oz tin pink salmon
200 g/7 oz tin tuna (in oil rather than brine)
3-4 tbsp fine matzo meal (available from some supermarkets which have a kosher section)
1 egg
1 onion
Parsley (optional)
Salt and pepper.

Drain the tin of salmon. Place the contents in a bowl and remove the bones and skin. Mix well with a fork. Drain the tin of tuna, add to the bowl and mix well. Add the raw egg and mix. Grate the onion onto the mixture (grating is best as it creates juice). Add some dried or fresh chopped parsley (optional), salt and pepper. Add enough matzo meal/flour to bind the mixture. Wet your hands, shake off excess water, and form patties, about the size of meatballs.

Heat the oil in a non-stick frying pan and test the heat by dropping in a few grains of flour. If they sizzle, then the heat is fine. Fill the frying pan with the patties (you may have to fry in batches). Cook on both sides until they are dark brown and arrange them around the sides of a colander to drain when cooked. This dish is nice with salad and mashed potato. The patties can be made to fit into pitta pockets or as finger food for a buffet.

Mohammed Majad Rashid recently obtained his Doctorate in our group. He says *'This recipe is from Dhangri shareef, Kashmir, Pakistan. It is normally cooked with minimal curry giving a dry dish, so that all the flavours of chicken and okra are intense. It is a succulent dish with soft mouth-watering okra – great with roti'.*

MAJAD'S CHICKEN AND OKRA CURRY

Serves 5 – 6

2-3 lb/900-1,350 g of chicken
1½ lb/675 g okra
3 medium sized onions
1 bulb of garlic
1½ green pepper
2 tomatoes
2 tsp tomato powder
2 tsp chilli powder (red)
1 tsp turmeric
2 tsp garam masala

Cut the onions roughly and place in a pan with the peeled garlic, pepper and some oil. Add salt to taste. Allow the onion/garlic mixture to sweat on low heat until soft. Add the tomato powder, chilli powder, turmeric and diced tomatoes and mix thoroughly.

Fry the spices for approximately 15 – 20 minutes, adding small amounts of water if necessary. Add the washed chicken and allow to cook for 5 minutes on a low heat. Turn up the heat and cook the chicken until tender. Always make sure that all the juices from the chicken have evaporated and that the chicken and spices are almost frying in the oil.

Wash the okra and drain. Pat dry with a towel and then top and tail the okra. Note that this should not be done before washing. Add the okra and garam masala to the chicken and mix thoroughly. Turn the heat down and cook on very low heat for 15 minutes or until okra is tender.

Garnish with fresh coriander and serve with rice or chapattis.

Finally, three more recipes from our research group. The first is contributed by Sarah Hankin. She says, 'I first served this vegetarian dish when I arranged a murder mystery dinner party, while I was studying at the University of Leicester. As my friends and I were busily cooking the meal, we didn't notice that the men were hatching a cunning plan. When the evening was drawing to a close, and the men were streets ahead of the girls in solving the mystery, they finally admitted that they had devised a secret system of cheating, by winking throughout the meal. Needless to say, the dish I recommend, murder mystery nights I do not'.

SARAH'S PENNE WITH QUORN IN A GARLIC AND WHITE WINE SAUCE

Serves 4

12 oz/350 g penne
2 tbsp butter
1 onion (chopped)
1 garlic clove (chopped)
1 bay leaf
425 ml/$^3/_4$ pint dry white wine
8 oz/225 g cooked quorn pieces
4 oz/110 g Gouda cheese, grated
1 tbsp chopped fresh mint
Salt and ground black pepper
150 ml/$^1/_4$ pint crème fraîche
Finely shredded fresh mint to garnish

Cook the pasta according to instructions. Heat the butter in a large frying pan and fry the onion for approximately 10 minutes, until softened. Stir in the garlic, bay leaf and wine and bring the contents to the boil. When the contents are reduced by about half, remove the bay leaf, stir in the crème fraîche and return to the boil.

Add the quorn pieces and Gouda cheese and simmer for 5 minutes, stirring occasionally until heated through. Add the chopped fresh mint and season to taste.

Finally, drain the pasta and turn it into a large serving dish. Add the sauce, garnish with finely shredded fresh mint and serve immediately.

The hospital in Gimbie, Ethiopia, which is Maternity Worldwide's headquarters in the country.

KIRSTE'S CHICKEN AND BACON TAGLIATELLE

Serves 4

200g/225 g fresh tagliatelle
1 chicken breast (cut into strips)
4 bacon rashers (cut into strips)
1 clove garlic (crushed)
½ onion (chopped)
1 glass white wine
200ml/7 fl oz tub creme fraiche
1 teaspoon fresh thyme leaves (finely chopped)

Cook the tagliatelle according to instructions and fry the bacon in 1 tbsp olive oil. Add the garlic and onion and cook until tender. Coat the chicken in about 2 tbsp flour, add to the pan and heat until cooked through, adding extra oil if necessary. Add the crème fraiche, white wine, thyme and salt and pepper and stir until crème fraiche has melted. Add the cooked tagliatelle and cook gently until the sauce has reduced.

RICHARD'S AROMATIC SPICED CHICK PEAS

Serves 4

250 g/9 oz dried chick peas
10-15 cherry tomatoes
1 whole pepper sliced (whatever colour)
1 inch/2.5 cm cubed piece of fresh ginger
3 cloves garlic
1-2 tbsp cumin seeds
1 tsp fennel seeds
½ tbsp ground coriander seeds
1 tsp turmeric
1-2 tbsp garam masala (not the variety with chilli) – this amount can be adjusted to taste
Salt and pepper to taste
10 tbsp sunflower oil and 4 tbsp olive oil (this amount can be adjusted to taste)

Soak the chick peas and boil until cooked. Drain and allow to cool. Roast the whole cherry tomatoes and strips of pepper in a hot oven (220°C/425°F/Gas Mark 7) until soft and juicy. When done, leave to cool.

Cut the ginger into small pieces and crush the garlic. Gently heat the sunflower oil and olive oil in a small pan, add the ginger to the oil and gently cook for 1 – 2 minutes. Next add the garlic, cumin seeds, fennel seeds, tumeric, garam masala, ground coriander seeds, salt and pepper.

Cook for a further 2 – 3 minutes, stirring as necessary. The seeds should go quite crispy (you can cook for more or less time depending on taste, just don't let the garlic burn). Pour the hot contents of the pan onto the chick peas, stir well, cover and leave for at least 30 minutes (overnight makes it even better).

Serve with roasted tomatoes and pepper with, if desired, soured cream, a sprinkle of lime juice, rocket leaves or chopped parsley.

The final recipe in this section was given to me by June Petit. She says *'This is my favourite sandwich filling because it tastes fabulous and I often make it when friends come for lunch. A great friend of mine invented it, so it has lots of good memories that go with it'*.

JUNE'S MOZZARELLA PESTO AND TOMATO ON OLIVE CIABATTA

1 olive ciabatta loaf
Green pesto
2 large tomatoes
1 – 2 buffalo mozzarella
Black pepper / salt

Slice through the ciabatta and spread the bottom with a generous layer of pesto. Slice the tomatoes and lay on top of the pesto. Grind black pepper next and a sprinkling of salt on tomatoes. Finally, layer with slices of mozzarella, about 1 cm/^{3}/$_8$ inch thick.

Replace the ciabatta lid, wrap the whole sandwich in foil and place in a hot oven for about 20 minutes until tomatoes have softened and cheese has melted. If it needs longer, pop back in the oven without the foil to lightly crisp the bread.

CHAPTER 8
THE USA

IN 1966, Stan and I went to live in Providence, Rhode Island, (between Boston and New York City), where Stan was carrying out post-doctoral research in Chemistry at Brown University. It was a wrench leaving family and friends behind in England and, in those days, it was too expensive to consider coming home for a visit. But I was excited at the prospect of life in America for a year and our journey there on the Queen Elizabeth I. It all turned out to be rather different from what I had expected. The five day trip on the QEI was no luxury cruise as it was the tail end of a hurricane. You could sit out on the lounger chairs on the deck, but only if you were covered by a blanket right up to the neck and swimming in the pool was quite a feat, because the depth of water varied from 1 foot to 6 feet within a few seconds, due to the pitching of the ship. Also, the ballroom dancing was an uphill and downhill affair. However, we made friends on the voyage, the meals were fantastic and eventually we arrived in New York.

As we came into the harbour, we saw the Statue of Liberty and then the towering skyscrapers of Manhattan. After the boat docked, our cabin trunks were deposited

Like thousands of others before us, this was our first view of the United States.

at various points on the quayside and it was our responsibility to track them all down, assemble them together and then find a customs official who would check them off. Then we found that it was a Jewish holiday, which meant that most of the taxis were not operating. Eventually after several more hours we found a taxi and arrived at our hotel for the night and the next day we set off on the rail trip through New England to Rhode Island. When we arrived in Providence, we were made very welcome by the Edwards family, Professor John Edwards who Stan was to work with, his wife Ruth and their two daughters, Kathy and Joan, until we could find an apartment.

As it was the end of September, the academic year had begun and all but one apartment had already been rented out. I had been dreaming of no washing up, with a dishwasher and all luxury appliances in a beautiful apartment. How different this was. We had to take a ground floor apartment on the corner which looked like the worst ever doctor's waiting room of those days. No two pieces of furniture matched, the lighting was very dim and only supplied by a few lamps and when you walked across the floor, even these lamps flickered and sometimes went out. The only gadget we found was a pencil sharpener, attached to the kitchen wall (presumably to sharpen your pencil, so you could more easily write down your list of complaints for the landlord). Eventually, 6 months later, we found a nicer apartment and moved in there.

I obtained a job in the Histology Department at the University, which also did not turn out to be what I had expected. I thought it would involve making microscope slides of plants or insects, but in fact I had to spend most of my time dissecting o'possum brains, cat brains and even human brains. I absolutely hated it and the only other person in the lab was the Professor's research assistant, Betty. In the weeks I was there, she only spoke to me once to let me know that, when she was my age, she worked in the Baltimore City Morgue and drank a fifth of whisky every day. Clearly I didn't measure up to her standards and she thought me a real wimp.

The next job I had was teaching chemistry in a high school about 30 miles away. This was quite interesting. I had to wear a badge marked 'STAFF' as many of the pupils looked as old or even older than I did. I only managed to keep this job for a few weeks because, when the school authorities checked up on my visa, they found that I was actually a 'Non-Resident Alien' and not entitled to work in the USA. After that I could only get casual work like child-minding, but there was usually plenty of that as Americans are very keen to have others look after their children (at least they were in those days). In fact, one lady went off to Vietnam for two weeks to visit her husband who was in the army there and left me her two year old twins to take care of.

One of the first things we did when we settled in in Rhode Island, was to find the local Methodist Church. On the first day we went there, we were made very welcome by the Minister, Ron Adcock and his wife Jo, who was also a Methodist Minister. We were invited to their home in the evening for dinner and left that evening having been appointed Youth Club Leaders. A youth club in USA in those days was quite different from anything we had known in the UK. The members were aged 15 and up and they met once every month to go on retreat, either to a Church guest house or to a private home which had been made available to them, by a member of the church or a friend. The young people would plan the catering themselves and we simply had to be there, organise the weekend programme and obtain speakers. So this was quite an interesting challenge.

After a few weeks, it was Thanksgiving (always the last Thursday in November) and Reverends Ron and Jo Adcock kindly invited us to their home to share in this most American of meals. Because it was a holiday, they suggested that we make a day or it and we arrived late morning as instructed, just to find that Jo was in bed with flu and out of action so far as Thanksgiving was concerned. However, she had left us written instructions on how to cook the dinner and other guests were due to arrive early evening. This was the first time I had cooked a roast turkey and pumpkin pie Thanksgiving dinner and you can imagine my shock at having to do this. Here is my recipe for Pumpkin Pie.

ANNE'S PUMPKIN PIE

Serves 8 - 10

1 cup sugar
1½-2 cups pumpkin, cut into pieces
½ tsp salt
½ tsp nutmeg
½ tsp ginger
½ tsp allspice
½ tsp cloves
1½ tsp cinnamon
1⅔ cups cream
2 eggs
9 inch/25 cm pastry pie case

Put the pumpkin pieces in a pan, add sufficient water to cover with a pinch of salt and cook until tender. Drain and mash the pumpkin. Add all ingredients and mix until smooth. Pour into a pie case and bake at 220°C/425°F/Gas Mark 7 for about 15 minutes. Then lower oven temperature to 180°C/350°F/Gas Mark 4 and bake pie for about 35 minutes more.

THE USA

When we had saved up enough money (it was impossible to get credit because we did not already have credit), we bought a car, a Ford Falcon station wagon, from one of Stan's colleagues, Mick Beallis who, with his wife Cami, had bought a sports car (not the most practical of transactions on their part as they had a new born baby). When it came to Christmas time a few weeks later, and Mick and Cami wanted to travel to their parents in Michigan and West Virginia respectively, they clearly had a problem, which they solved at a stroke by inviting us to go along with them (and use the station wagon). First we went to Cami's parents for Christmas and it was an interesting journey – about 500 miles in a snowstorm and then we went on to Mick's parents for New Year at Sarnia near Detroit (very industrialised). However, we did have the opportunity to drive to Niagara and see the falls partially frozen and the spray freezing on the iron railings making fascinating patterns. The wintry scenery in New England, was very beautiful.

We did have some wonderful times in USA and made many friends. In the autumn we took a weekend to drive up to New Hampshire and Vermont to see the fall foliage and the colours were absolutely amazing – better than we had imagined. We also used to drive out to the apple orchards in Rhode Island and pick our own apples and there were lots of wayside fruit stalls, with pumpkins for sale (then almost unknown in the UK).

To our surprise we found that many beaches in USA are private, but Brown University had a beach called Haffenreffer Grant and we often went there to picnic or barbecue. It was fun fishing off the rocks for Striped Bass. Another place we enjoyed very much was Newport, Rhode Island, with many beautiful yachts and homes. We once went to the famous Newport Jazz Festival - at least as far as the car park – entry to the Festival itself was much too expensive for us at that time. So we joined groups of students and sat on the roof of our car, listening to the music.

We spent a lot of time with the Edwards, who made us very welcome. Ruth was from the mid-west and an expert cook. Before Christmas, we went to their home and helped them decorate the tree and it was there that, for the first time, we heard the carol 'Deck the Halls with Boughs of Holly' and really found it a wonderful carol. We enjoyed many delicious meals at the Edwards' house and I include here Ruth's recipe for brownies, a great American favourite.

The author skiing at Heavenly, California, with Lake Tahoe in the background.

RUTH'S BROWNIES

Makes about 30 brownies

4 oz/110 g unsweetened chocolate
1 tsp vanilla
1¼ cups self raising flour
2 cups sugar
4 eggs
1 cup chopped nuts (pecan or walnuts)
⅔ cup shortening

Heat oven to (180°C/350°F/Gas Mark 4) and grease baking pan, approximately 13 inch x 9 inch x 2 inch (30 cm x 20 cm x 5 cm). Melt the chocolate and shortening in a large saucepan over low heat. Remove from the heat and mix in sugar, eggs and vanilla. Stir in remaining ingredients and spread in the pan.

Bake for 30 minutes or until brownies start to pull away from the sides of the pan. Do not over bake. Cool slightly, then cut into bars about 2 inch x 1½ inch (5 cm x 4 cm). If desired, spread with glossy chocolate frosting (icing) before cutting.

We also spent quite a lot of time with the Smith family, from Matthewson Street Church, Norman and Lola and their children Warren, Scudder and Rachel. The children loved to go to the Newport Creamery and order an 'Awful-Awful' which was rather awful. It consisted of 4 scoops of ice cream, syrup and Coca Cola.

Whilst at Brown University, I was a member of the ladies group 'Sepia' with my friend Susan Barnhill. It was a good way of meeting new people and sharing new experiences. There was an English Conversation Group where I had the task of helping foreign students to learn 'proper' English. I will always remember the end of term dinner which the Gourmet Cook section of Sepia and the English Conversation Group held for partners. The menu was decided by the Committee and people rapidly volunteered to make/bring the easier items. Suddenly I found I had been left with preparing the Beef stroganoff. This was the first time this gourmet had ever heard of stroganoff. Later I became quicker at volunteering to bring the garlic bread. But there was a consolation. Susan provided me with the recipe for beef stroganoff and here it is. I still make it from time to time. The key to success is to buy good quality beef and it is a good idea to consult your butcher.

ANNE'S BEEF STROGANOFF

Serves 4

1 lb/450 g boneless chuck, sirloin or top round steak
2 tbsp olive oil
2 tbsp butter
1 cup chopped onion
1½ cups sliced mushrooms
1 can consommé
Dash of nutmeg
1 tsp salt
2 cups sour cream
2 tbs flour
8 oz/225 g wide egg noodles

Trim off any excess fat from the meat and slice into thin strips. Heat the oil. Add onion, mushrooms and the meat. Brown for 10 minutes, add the consommé and simmer, the longer the better (at least 30 minutes). Just before serving, add sour cream mixed with flour and salt and the cooked, drained egg noodles., heat and serve immediately.

At the end of the year, we produced a cook book, called 'Sepia Cooks' and I have included some recipes from my friends, Betty Grourke and Susan Barnhill. I have remained friends with Susan ever since and have seen her frequently on my visits to the USA. This is her recipe for turkey soup and when we say goodbye to the Christmas turkey, I make a pan of this delicious soup every year.

SUSAN'S TURKEY AND VEGETABLE SOUP

Makes around 8 pints/4 litres

Bones and trimmings from 1 turkey (not the skin)
3 chicken stock cubes
1½ tsp salt (or more)
1-2 bay leaves
¼ tsp poultry seasoning
¼ cup cooked chopped turkey
¼ cup chopped parsley
1 cup finely diced carrots
1 cup finely diced celery
2 medium onions (chopped)
1 lb/450 g can tomatoes
6-8 oz/175-225 g egg noodles

Break the bones up into pieces that will fit into the pan (large pressure cooker size). Cook them for as long as you wish with some of the onion, salt and bay leaves and cover them with water and simmer. Cool the broth somewhat so that you can handle the bones, then either strain the bones from the broth or pick them out by hand, making sure that all small bones are found. I have found a combination of these methods works best. If you wish you may pick the meat from the bones or discard it. I like to wash and dry the pan, and strain the stock into it and add everything but the noodles. Cook for an additional 45 minutes, then add the noodles and boil for 10 minutes more. Season to taste. The soup freezes well.

A good accompaniment to this soup is French or Italian bread that has been buttered and sprinkled with parmesan cheese and grilled.

It is 46 years since I saw Betty, but we still keep in touch. Here is her recipe for 'Country Chicken'.

BETTY'S COUNTRY CHICKEN

Serves 4-6.

¼ cup butter
3 lb/1.5 kg chicken (in pieces)
2 onions
1 clove garlic
2 strips bacon
½ cup cider
1 Bouillon (stock) cube
¼ tsp salt
Dash pepper
Few sprigs parsley
1 Bay leaf
3 medium onions
3 medium carrots
2 small turnips
½ cup peas, fresh or frozen

Melt half the butter in a skillet, add the chicken pieces and fry over a medium heat until golden. Set aside. Sauté finely chopped onions, chopped garlic and bacon cut into pieces in a medium saucepan. Add cider, Bouillon (stock) cube dissolved in ½ cup of boiling water, salt, pepper, parsley and bay leaf. Simmer for a few minutes.

Add chicken, cover and bake in a pre-heated oven at (160°C/325°F/Gas Mark 2-3) for about 1 hour or until tender. Fifteen minutes before serving, melt remaining butter in a saucepan and add onions, carrots and turnips, all sliced thinly. Add peas along with ¼ cup of the chicken broth. Cover and cook over low heat, stirring occasionally, until vegetables are tender. Serve vegetables spooned around the chicken.

Here are another couple of traditional American recipes from the 'Sepia' book.

BEEF AND VEGETABLES, CHINESE STYLE

Serves 4

1 lb/450 g good quality beef steak
4 tsp soy sauce
1 tsp cornstarch
1 tbsp dry sherry
1 sliced ginger root
1 tsp sugar
4-5 tbsp oil
½ tsp salt,
2 cups green vegetables (e.g. snow peas (mange-tout) and Chinese cabbage)
1 cup various other vegetables (e.g. mushrooms, bean sprouts, bamboo shoots, water chestnuts)

Cut the meat into 2 inch x ¼ inch (5 cm x 0.5 cm) strips and marinate it in the first five ingredients above for 15 minutes. Heat 2 tbsp of the oil in a pan and lightly fry the vegetables. Then remove from the pan and set aside. Add more oil to the pan with salt and fry the marinated meat. Then add the vegetables again and heat. Serve immediately over hot rice.

CRÈME WAFERS (From Sweden)

Yields approximately 40.

1 cup butter
⅓ cup milk
2 cups flour

Filling (icing)
¼ cup butter
¾ cup sifted icing sugar

Mix butter, milk and flour and chill overnight. Roll out dough (small portions at a time to about ⅛ inch (¼ cm) thickness and cut into round or square shapes about 1¼ inches/3 cm across. Dip each piece into a bowl of sugar, coating it completely and then place on a greased biscuit sheet. Then pierce 3-4 times with a fork so that it does not puff up too much. Bake at 180°C/350°F/Gas Mark 4 for 8-10 minutes or until slightly browned. Make the filling (icing) by creaming the butter and icing sugar together and spreading on top of the wafers.

Jelloed salads (salad or vegetables, presented in a mould of gelatine) are very popular in America, possibly because they can be made in advance and can be transported very easily. I can well remember taking a trifle, being a traditional British dessert, to a church pot luck supper. I was amazed to see it served alongside the hotpots, in mistake for one of these jelloed salads. However, the people having the hot pot seemed to enjoy the trifle eaten at the same time, including the custard and the whipped double cream!

A nice jelloed salad is an attractive garnish to a fish dish and here is a traditional recipe.

VEGETABLE TRIO JELLOED SALAD

Makes about 6 cups or 12 individual side salads.

2 packets (3 oz/80 g each) lemon jelly (jello in American English)
1 tbsp salt
2 cups boiling water
2 cups cold water
2 tbsp vinegar
1½ cups finely shredded carrots
1¾ cups finely shredded cabbage
1 tsp minced chives
1½ cups finely chopped spinach

Dissolve the jelly and salt in boiling water. Add cold water and vinegar. Chill until slightly thickened, then divide into three portions. Fold carrots into one portion, pour into a 9 inch x 5 inch x 3 inch (25 cm x 13 cm x 10 cm) loaf tin or similar. Chill until set, but not firm. Fold cabbage into second portion, pour into the tin and chill until set but not firm. Fold chives and spinach into remaining jelly, pour this third layer into the tin and chill until firm. Turn out of the tin, then slice and garnish with crisp greens.

While we were in the USA, transatlantic flights to England were becoming popular and more affordable, so we had several visitors from England. Stan's parents came to stay with us and also friends, John Weatherson, Brenda Nicholson and Stan's brother, Melvyn. At that time a world exhibition, EXPO 67 was on in Montreal, about 400 miles from Providence. They all seemed to want to go to visit it and also to Niagara Falls, so we spent a good deal of time driving the circular route to Montreal, Niagara and then back to Providence, but it was fun.

By September it was time to come home. This time, we decided to try the new air travel and shipped our cabin trunks on the Queen Elizabeth, but flew back home. In the meantime, the dock workers went on strike at Southampton and we were left until nearly Christmas without our winter clothes. So all in all, it was a very memorable visit to the USA.

In the late 70s we were lucky enough to be able to spend three summers on Cape Cod in a little place called Woods Hole. Stan was working at the Marine Biology Laboratory, where scientists from all of the USA and other countries would go to do research. We stayed in a little wooden cottage in the woods and each summer, the same people were in the same cottages, so we got to know them well. The children enjoyed it very much. They had swimming lessons on the beach from the lifeguard, went to the Children's School of Science and enjoyed exploring the saltwater pools and seeing horseshoe crabs. They also played tennis.

Some scientists worked on Goosefish, rather strangely shaped fish with massive heads in proportion to the bodies. It turned out that these fish had an organ that secreted an insulin-like substance and so could be used as a model to study insulin production and diabetes. On Thursday evenings, the families of those who worked on goosefish had 'Goosefish Suppers' where each family would try a different recipe with the goosefish. In the UK today, we know these fish as 'Monkfish' and they have become a popular dish in restaurants. Monkfish (especially the tails) are now readily available in the UK at supermarkets and fishmongers. Our friend Stella Murdoch has kindly supplied the following recipe.

STELLA'S MONKFISH PARCELS

Serves 4

1 large monkfish tail cut into 4 portions without the backbone
1 carrot cut into thin strips
4 spring onions, cut into thin strips
1 inch root ginger peeled and cut into very thin strips
Salt and black pepper
4 sheets non-stick parchment/baking or greaseproof paper

Sauce
1 tsp honey
2 tsp sesame oil
1 tbsp soy sauce
2 tbsp white wine

Lay out each sheet of paper and in the centre, share out the strips of vegetable and ginger and top with a fish portion. Start a parcel with the ends of the paper and pour the sauce in to each parcel. Season the fish and then fold up the paper to provide a seal both ways and secure with a paper clip.

Place on a grill pan/roasting dish and cook for 30 minutes at 170°C/335°F/Gas Mark 3. Serve each parcel on a plate, but do not undo the paper clip until ready to eat. Serve with rice or with rosti potatoes.

JOAN'S TUSCANY CHICKEN

Serves 4

One 1½ - 2 lb (700 – 900 g) chicken
½ lemon
1 tbsp olive oil
4 or 5 cloves of garlic, crushed or roughly sliced
Big sprig of rosemary

Optional
4 tbsp yogurt
2 tbsp soy sauce

Make a paste of the yogurt/soy sauce mixture and rub the inside of the chicken with it. Squeeze some lemon juice, add some garlic cloves and one large sprig of rosemary into the cavity of the chicken.

With your hands gently lift up the skin of the chicken and slip some garlic cloves, lemon peel, and a few leaves of rosemary under the skin. Rub the olive oil on the chicken.

Roast the chicken, in a covered roasting pan, at very high heat (220°C/425°F/Gas Mark 7) for 20 minutes. Then turn the heat very low (120°C/250°F/Gas Mark 1) and cook the chicken slowly for about 1 to 1½ hours. Fifteen minutes before serving, turn up the heat very high (220°C/425°F/Gas Mark 7) for final browning/crisping.

Pour off juices, remove all fat. The brown sauce may be served as is. It is very intense and delicious.

Much of Ethiopia is at high altitude and nights can be cold, so Maternity Worldwide's baby vests are much in demand.

JOAN'S LOW FAT RISOTTO

Serves 4

1 cup rice (Uncle Bens extra long grain not instant), Balsamic (Indian) or Arobio (Italian)
1 tsp olive oil
1-2 cloves of garlic
½ small onion
½ cup white wine (optional)
Chicken broth (Campbell's if possible)

Gently fry the garlic and onion in olive oil. Do not brown. Add the dry rice and make certain that each grain is covered in olive oil. Add chicken broth, some water, and/or white wine. Bring to a boil and then turn the heat down very low and cook for about 20 minutes.

It tastes fattening and creamy, but you can add parmesan at the end if you want to. You may also add a small pat of butter (at the end) if you want a buttery taste.

For mushroom Risotto, use a mixture of mushrooms when you sauté the garlic/onions.

For seafood Risotto, add seafood (clams or shrimp or crab) in the last 5 minutes. You can substitute some of the chicken broth with clam broth.

CHAPTER 9
INTERNATIONAL

Because of my husband's job, I've had the opportunity to travel widely and to meet people from countries throughout the world, so this chapter is devoted to recipes from friends in many different countries.

Vanda Hatziconstantinou came to England from Greece with her husband, Haris, who was to become one of Stan's PhD students. This was in the early 70s and we've kept in touch with them ever since. I include her recipe for a cherry liqueur. The recipe needs sunshine, which is in good supply in Greece, but it would be worth trying anywhere. Vanda says *'This is a liqueur which is really aromatic and full of flavour. Here in Greece, we traditionally used to offer Kerasso to visitors along with a piece of chocolate as a welcome'*.

VANDA'S KERASSO (SOUR CHERRY LIQUEUR)

Yields about 2 pints/1,100 ml of liqueur
2 lb/900 g sour cherries
2 lb/900 g sugar
10 whole cloves
2 cinnamon sticks in pieces
1 pint/½ litre good quality brandy

Wash the cherries thoroughly and remove the stems. Rinse one more time and leave them to drain in a colander. Put the cherries into a wide-mouthed bottle and add the sugar and spices. Cover tightly with a piece of cloth and fasten it well round the neck of the bottle. Use a plastic membrane to cover it additionally. Shake the bottle from time to time. Allow to macerate in a sunny place for about 40 days. When the sugar has dissolved completely, drain the cherry juice, which is now full of flavour, through a coffee filter and mix the juice you receive from the filter with the brandy. Keep the liqueur in a nice bottle from which it can be served.

I've known the Heirwegh family also since the 1970s. Karel Heirwegh and his wife Dora have seven children, and I always remember the first time we visited. All of the children were lined up in age order and introduced to us – 'Sound of Music' style. One of the children (now all grown up) is Piet Heirwegh. I include recipes from Dora and Piet.

DORA'S RIB OF PORK

Serves 6

6 pork chops
Mustard
Caster sugar
Butter
Squeezed oranges
Whole oranges
Potato flour
Large glass Grand Marnier

Place pork ribs in an oven-proof dish and sprinkle with pepper and salt to taste. Cover with a layer of ½ cm/¼ inch of mustard, caster sugar and some pieces of butter. Place in a pre-heated oven (220°C/425°F/Gas Mark 7) for 1 hour per 1 kg/ 2 lb of meat. At regular intervals, pour juice from several oranges over the meat.

About 15 minutes before the meat is ready, pour Grand Marnier over the meat. Peel additional oranges (1 per person) and cut in slices. Cut the meat, lay in a heated serving dish and put slices of oranges around the meat. Place the rest of the sliced orange into the original meat dish with remaining cooking juices and thicken the sauce with potato flour.

Cover the meat with part of the sauce and serve the rest of the sauce separately in a gravy boat. Serve with mashed potatoes or bread.

The Bay of Fundy (in the Maritime Provinces of Canada, see p 106) has the world's highest tides, with obvious problems for mooring boats.

This bell tower is in Buenos Aires, one of the world's most elegant cities.

PIET'S CRISPED CHICORY WITH HAM AND CHEESE

Serves 4.

8 strips of Parma ham
chicory heads
Double cream
Gruyère or Parmesan cheese
Butter
Plain flour
Milk
Salt and pepper

Boil the chicory in salted water and let it drain well. Make a cheese sauce from butter, flour, milk, pepper, salt, cream and grated cheese.

Wind the ham around the chicory and place in an oven-proof dish. Pour the sauce over, sprinkle with further grated cheese and add small pieces of butter. Place in a pre-heated oven (220°C/400°F/Gas Mark 6) for 15 minutes and then crisp under the grill.

Francesco De Matteis is originally from Italy, though he has lived in England for many years. We've met up many times at conferences and he has visited us at home. I include his recipe for a risotto.

FRANCESCO'S RISOTTO A LA MILANESE

Serves 4 – 6

½ tsp saffron
1 small onion (chopped)
1000 ml/¾ pint of chicken stock (can be prepared by dissolving 2 chicken cubes in water)
350 g/12 oz Arborio rice
75 g/3 oz butter
100 g/4 oz freshly grated Parmesan cheese

Dissolve the saffron in a small cup of warm stock. Heat half the butter in a deep frying pan, add the onion and cook gently until golden in colour. Add half the saffron stock to the rice and blend thoroughly by stirring constantly with a wooden spoon. Add the rest of the stock, a ladleful at a time, waiting for the rice to absorb the stock and stirring all the time. When the rice is done, tender but firm to the bite, add the Parmesan cheese and the rest of the butter. Mix thoroughly and serve hot.

Although I have never been to Argentina, I met Alcira Batlle de Albertoni, from Buenos Aires, at conferences abroad and she has been a frequent visitor to our home in Yorkshire. I include her recipe for 'Dulce de Leche', of which she says *'Most Argentine desserts use dulce de leche, it is the national obsession. About 120,000 tons of dulce de leche are made today, of which 4,000 tons are exported. Often if not always, Argentineans travelling abroad take dulce de leche in their lugagge, as a typical present and for their own use. At the beginning, foreigners might think it is far too sweet, but after a short while, they become equally passionate about it'.*

ALCIRA'S DULCE DE LECHE

1,000 ml/1 $^{3}/_{4}$ pints milk
350 g/12 oz sugar dissolved in 150 ml/ $^{1}/_{4}$ pint of hot water.
$^{1}/_{2}$ vanilla pod
Pinch of bicarbonate of soda

Add the milk and bicarbonate of soda to a saucepan (copper if possible) and boil, then add the sugar and vanilla. Allow the mixture to boil gently for 50 minutes, with constant stirring, using a long-handled wooden spoon. Special attention and care should be paid to avoid the mixture burning or sticking. The preparation must reach the caramel colour (light brown). When the mix is ready, continue stirring until it cools down. If one wishes this step to be speeded up, the copper saucepan can be put into another saucepan or tin filled with cold water.

Sampans once almost covered Hong Kong harbour, but are now less common.

I regularly meet Julia Levy at conferences throughout Europe and have also visited her several times in Vancouver, Canada where she lives. Julia is an internationally-known scientist, but also a highly successful businesswoman, having pioneered the development of a new drug for preventing blindness. She sent me a delicious recipe for a barbecued salmon. She says *'this dish can be served with a variety of fresh buttered vegetables or a garden salad and is delicious with cous cous or pilaf. It is one of our summer favorites when fresh wild salmon are readily available on the west coast of Canada'*.

JULIA'S CHILLI-BARBECUED SALMON WITH MANGO SALSA

Serves 4 - 6

1½ lb/675 g salmon fillet (skin on)
2 tbsp chilli oil (or substitute 2 tbsp olive oil plus hot pepper sauce to taste)
2 tbsp lime juice (better fresh but not essential)
2 tbsp chopped cilantro (coriander)
1 tbsp grated fresh ginger
2 garlic cloves, minced
Mango salsa
1 medium tomato diced
1 mango peeled and diced
¼ cup chopped green (spring) onion
1 tbsp of marinade mixture from above
Salt and pepper to taste

Mix together all ingredients except salmon in a small bowl. Reserve 1 tbsp of the mixture to season the salsa (see below). Put the remaining mixture in a flat dish, large enough to place the salmon in, flesh side down. Allow it to marinate for about 30 minutes.

Heat the barbecue to medium high and oil the grill. Sear salmon flesh side down for about 3 minutes, turn over, and cook the salmon until it flakes when tested with a fork. Salmon should still be quite pink at the centre for best tasting fish. Length of cooking varies with thickness of fillet but is usually between 5-10 minutes.

The salsa is simply made by stirring in all the ingredients and then can either be layered on top of the salmon or served in a separate bowl.

Carolyn and Roy Pottier are good friends who live in Kingston, Ontario, Canada in a beautiful area of the St Lawrence River, known as the 'Thousand Islands'. (Yes, it is the place where the, now famous, salad dressing originated). We have visited their home several times and Carolyn made the following salad for us, which was delicious. Carolyn says *'This salad originated from the Maritime Provinces of Canada, which include Nova Scotia and New Brunswick, where I came from before moving to Kingston. The addition of grated peel and orange liqueur makes this a delicious salad. Enjoy!'*

CAROLYN'S ORANGE & ALMOND SALAD

Serves 6.
¼ cup olive oil
1 tsp sugar
1 tbsp cider vinegar
2 tsp grated orange peel
4 tbsp orange juice concentrate
4 tbsp orange liqueur
Assorted iceberg, Romaine lettuce or baby spinach leaves to serve 6
1 small can (10 oz/284 ml) orange segments (drained)
¼ cup slivered almonds

Mix together the oil, sugar, vinegar, orange peel, juice and liqueur. Clean, rinse and dry the lettuce leaves, break up and place in a large bowl. Pour sauce over and lightly toss. Garnish with mandarin slices and a sprinkle of slivered almonds.

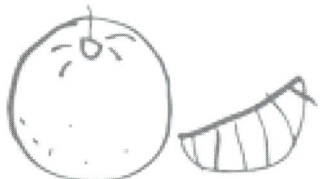

I was fortunate enough to be able to accompany Stan when he went to work in Auckland, New Zealand for six weeks. We stayed with Paula and Colin Green (Colin was a research collaborator with Stan). We had planned to stay with a dermatologist in Auckland, but this arrangement fell through at the last moment and Colin and Paula very kindly stepped into the breach. They were most hospitable, and even lent us their red sports car to go touring at weekends. I include some recipes from Paula who said: *'Because the book is for Maternity Worldwide, it seemed appropriate to include recipes that were obtained from mothers. Here are three recipes; each a family favourite passed down'.*

PAULA'S PEANUT BROWNIES

1½ cups flour
1 cup sugar
¼ lb/110 g butter (melted)
1 egg
A little vanilla essence
1 cup peanuts (roasted)
½ tsp salt
2 tsp cocoa
½ tsp baking powder

Beat the sugar and egg and add to the butter and mix well. Add the vanilla essence. Sift in the dry ingredients and mix well. Mix in the peanuts. Use a teaspoon to form biscuit shapes on a clean oven tray. Bake in the middle of the oven at 180°C/350°F/Gas Mark 4 for 20 minutes.

PAULA'S BRUSSELS CAKE

¼ lb/110 g butter
¼ lb/110 g sugar
½ lb/225 g self raising flour
1 egg
A pinch of salt
Jam or fruit (for filling)

Whiz all ingredients together in a food processor. Press half the mixture into an 8 or 9 inch (20 cm or 25 cm) cake tin. Spread a layer of jam or fruit over this base. Sprinkle the rest of the crumb mixture on top and bake for approximately 35 minutes at 180°C/350°F/Gas Mark 4.

PAULA'S DATE BALLS

3 oz/80 g butter
½ cup sugar
1 small egg (beaten)
1 cup chopped dates
½ tsp vanilla essence
1 cup rice bubbles (puffed rice or rice crispies)

Put the above ingredients into a saucepan and heat, stirring all the time. Boil for 3 minutes, then allow to cool. Mix in 1 cup of rice bubbles.

Use a teaspoon and wet hands to roll into balls, then dip these in desiccated coconut or chocolate chips. Keep in refrigerator until required.

Hong Kong is one of my favourite places to visit. Of, course, the shopping is legendary, but I just enjoy the whole atmosphere. There is always so much going on. On my first visit we stayed in the New World Harbour View Hotel and, when we entered our room on the 32nd floor, I just could not take in the view. It was staggering. One wall was just a window from floor to ceiling and it looked out over the whole harbour with a host of big ships, junks and little sampans moving everywhere. At the other side of the harbour was the famous (or perhaps infamous) Kai Tak airport, where we watched jumbo jets turning between blocks of flats on their final approach, before landing.

The pace of change in Hong Kong is amazing. Now they have a new airport and a huge number of new buildings. The New World Hotel is still there, but it can no longer justify the title 'Harbour View' as the harbour has been partly filled in and several taller buildings constructed in front.

We have many Chinese friends in Hong Kong, among them the Mok family who we see quite often either in Hong Kong or in Leeds. Maisie Mok has given me this recipe for steamed fish, which is a favourite in Hong Kong. Maisie explains why steaming is used so much in Chinese dishes, especially fish.

'Steaming is a very popular way of cooking fish in Southern China. Rice wine, ginger, hot pepper and peanut oil are used to mask or take away the fishy smell and taste in the fish while other ingredients are for adding flavour to the dish. Controlling the time is very important in steaming fish since it will determine whether the fish is correctly cooked or over-cooked. The former gives tender flesh while the latter a tough texture. As a simple test of whether the fish is cooked, try inserting the point of a knife or a fork into the fish – if the knife/fork goes through the flesh easily, the fish is cooked through.

Steaming preserves the best taste and tenderness of the fish. By using simple ingredients and steam as the means of cooking, it demands the freshest materials and highest command of the timing and it offers a very delicious dish which is also good for health'.

MAISIE'S STEAMED FISH – CHINESE STYLE

Perch, bass, carp, bream, trout, mackerel, sole or snapper can be used.
Serves 4 – 6

1 fish weighing about 700g/1½ lb
2 – 4 slices ginger root
1 – 2 red hot peppers
Cornstarch
Rice wine or gin
2 tbsp peanut oil
1 tbsp light soy sauce
25 g/1oz raw pork
2 Chinese celery stalks with leaves, or celery heart cut into
4 cm/1½ inch pieces
2 large Chinese dried mushrooms, soaked and stems removed
2 – 4 stalks spring onions (scallions)
Some parsley

Scale and gut the fish, clean and dry well. Trim off fins and tail. If the fish is thick, about 4 cm/1½ inches, score the body three or four times half way down on both sides. Place the fish on an oblong dish and spread a thin layer of cornstarch on the top. Add chopped hot pepper and shredded ginger root, raw pork, Chinese mushroom and celery over it.

Bring 1,000 ml/1¾ pints water to the boil in a wok. Put a wire rack in the wok and set the dish on top. Sprinkle rice wine on the fish and steam vigorously over a high heat for 7 – 10 minutes only.

Remove the dish of fish from the wok, drain and set aside. Place chopped spring onion and the parsley on the fish. Heat peanut oil to boiling in a pan. Pour the oil over the fish followed by the light soy sauce along the sides. Serve hot.

Variations to this recipe could include adding either a tablespoon of black bean sauce with a tablespoon of finely chopped garlic or two tablespoons of salted mustard vegetable sauce (available from Chinese supermarkets). For either of these variations the spring onion and parsley may be omitted.

I met Kathy and Patrick Davey when we first came to Leeds to live. Patrick was working at Leeds University with Stan. They moved to Ireland soon afterwards, where we kept in touch and more recently they have move to live in Uganda, where Patrick is Vice-Chancellor at the University of Mountains of the Moon. Kathy has provided two recipes and says *'This jelly recipe is ideal for lazy people with a freezer! The basic idea is to use a packet of jelly with half the usual amount of water and add frozen fruit and sugar to taste. It then sets very quickly'.*

KATHY'S JELLY IN A JIFFY

1 packet raspberry jelly
½ pint/275 ml boiling water
1 tbsp sugar
8 oz/225 g frozen (or tinned) raspberries

Dissolve the jelly and sugar in boiling water and then add frozen raspberries. Stir gently until the raspberries have thawed. Leave to set. You can use tinned raspberries but you will need less water and less sugar. To speed up setting time, you can add ice cubes with the fruit.
  Variations: Orange jelly with gooseberry purée.
       Lemon jelly with rind and juice of a lemon and apple purée.
  To any variation you can add some cold custard and liquidise with the mix and froth up. To make a richer dessert, when the jelly is really setting, fold in some whipped cream (½ pint/275 ml). In this case, use a little less water with the jelly.

Kathy also gave me this recipe for using up cheese.

KATHY'S BEST BEFORE CHEESE SPREAD

'Old' or sour cream
Past 'best before' cheese(s)
Dried herbs to taste

The proportion of cheese to cream depends on the cheese(s) i.e. harder cheeses need less cream. Add all the ingredients to a small saucepan and stir over a good heat until melded. Pour over toast/bread and allow to soak in.

It is interesting how I came to meet Jean and Rod McArthur, from Kyabram, not far from Melbourne in Australia. We were on a flight back from the US, when their daughter, Raelene, sat next to me on the flight. By the end of the flight we had made friends and we kept in touch. When we went to a conference in Melbourne, her parents came to meet us and took us out for a most interesting meal of Moreton Bay Bugs, a seafood delicacy from the region. They were the ugliest items of food I have ever come across, but if you did not concentrate on their appearance, but on their taste, they were very acceptable. Jean and Rod have visited us several times at our home in Yorkshire and I include two of Jean's recipes. Jean tells how the first of these arose

'In the early days of colonial Australia, there was no yeast and the first settlers lacked the knowledge to make a substitute, so they made 'Damper', an unleavened bread cooked in the coals of a camp fire or open fireplace'.

JEAN'S DAMPER

3 cups SR flour
30 g/1 oz butter
½ cup milk

Rub the butter into the flour, add the milk and enough water to mix to a sticky dough. Knead lightly. Place on a greased tray, slash the top with a knife and brush with milk or water. Bake in a moderately hot oven for 30 minutes or until the damper sounds hollow. Break open and serve hot with butter and syrup or jam or honey. It is best used immediately after cooking.

JEAN'S AUSTRALIAN MEAT PIES

Makes 8 individual pies.

Filling
750 g/1½ lb minced beef
2 beef stock cubes
Salt
2 tbsp plain flour
3½ cups water
1 tsp soy sauce

Base Pastry
2 cups plain flour
½ tsp salt
⅔ cup water
60 g/2 oz dripping

Brown the minced beef and add the stock cubes, 2 cups of water and salt and heat. Stir until boiling, reduce the heat, cover and simmer for 20 minutes. Thicken with plain flour and 1½ cups water and soy sauce.

Make pastry in the traditional way with the ingredients above. Roll out and line 8 small pie tins. Fill with meat mixture and top with Ruff Puff pastry (this can be purchased ready-made). Prick the centres of the pies. Bake at 200°C/400°F/Gas Mark 6 for 5 minutes, then reduce to 180°C/350°F/Gas Mark 4. Cook for another 10 minutes.

Janet Ihenacho is the sister of a very good friend of mine and lived in Nigeria for many years, where she raised her family. I only met her recently since she came back to live in the UK and she gave me the following recipe for Jollof Rice. Janet says ' *this spicy rice dish is a favourite in Nigeria and other West African countries. It is traditionally served on special occasions such as birthdays, Christmas etc and may be served hot or cold*'.

JANET'S JOLLOF RICE

Serves 4

1 onion
1 bell pepper
1 tin tomatoes (or fresh tomatoes)
2 tbsp oil (eg sunflower or corn)
2 cups long-grained rice

Process the onion, pepper and tomatoes in a liquidiser or food processor. In a saucepan, add this vegetable purée to the oil and heat with stirring to form a thick, richly coloured sauce. Add the rice to this sauce, add salt to taste and sufficient water to cook the rice. It is better to add the water gradually, adding more as needed as the rice will not be strained.

Boil the rice for about 20 minutes until cooked. The rice should be moist, but not wet, having absorbed the sauce. For added flavour, a stock cube and some tomato purée may be added to the cooking rice. This is usually served with chicken pieces or cubes of beef. For a vegetarian dish, quartered hard-boiled eggs may be substituted for the meat.

A traditional accompaniment is fried plantain. If you have never tasted this food, Janet recommends that you do. Plantain looks like a very large banana, but must be cooked. After peeling, the plantain is cut diagonally into slices and fried in oil.

CHAPTER 10
FAMILY FAVOURITES

FINALLY, this chapter contains just a few favourites of my own family. I have always enjoyed making soups of all different kinds and here are two which are a little out of the ordinary, but which are really delicious.

ANNE'S AVOCADO SOUP

1 ripe avocado
1 small green pepper seeded and chopped
25 g/1 oz butter
25 g/1 oz) flower
150 ml/$^1/_2$pint) milk
1 litre/1$^3/_4$ pints chicken stock
Salt and pepper to season

First make a roux by melting the butter in a heavy based sauce pan, stir in the flour slowly and cook gently for 2-3 minutes, taking care not to brown the roux. Remove from the heat and add the milk whilst stirring continuously. Gradually add the stock along with the green pepper and seasoning. Simmer covered for 15 minutes.

Mash the flesh from the avocado to a smooth cream in a small basin. Add some of the stock to the avocado to even consistency. Add the avocado into the main pan of stock. Simmer the soup but do not boil it.

Allow to cool a little and then liquidise (a handheld liquidiser is ideal, but a food processor or blender can be used). Return to the pan and bring to serving temperature, stirring frequently.

This is a really great recipe for using up an avocado which may be too soft for use in a salad. Serve with herb croutons

ANNE'S BUTTERNUT SQUASH SOUP

1 large butternut squash, peeled, seeds removed and diced
1 small onion finely chopped
1-2 cloves of garlic finely chopped
1 tbsp olive oil
1 litre/1^3/$_4$ pints of chicken or vegetable stock

Pour the oil into a large heavy based pan and when hot add the onion and cook until soft and brown. Add the garlic and continue to cook for a further 2-3 minutes.

Add cubes of butternut squash and turn in the pan for two minutes. Drain off any excess oil, add stock and bring to the boil and simmer for 20 minutes until the butternut squash is tender. Allow to cool a little and then liquidise (a handheld liquidiser is ideal, but a food processor or blender can be used). Return to the pan and bring to serving temperature, stirring frequently.

This is a delicious sweet soup and has always been very popular where I have served it. You may want to serve with croutons or crusty bread.

Last year, as a fundraising idea with a difference for Maternity Worldwide, my son Adrian and his Scottish friend and neighbour Atholl, hosted a 'Burn's Night Banquet'. It was a lavish affair which included 22 guests seated on a long table draped in tartan in Atholl's home (fortunately he has a very large living room). Attention to detail (and lots of whisky) ensured it was a great success. One couple there commented that they had enjoyed it even more than their recent wedding. I have included the menu and programme below, and a selection of some of the recipes. A recipe for Atholl Brose has already been included in Chapter 7. At the Burn's Banquet this was particularly fitting given the name of the host. A slight variation on the recipe was used adding raspberries to the cream, replacing the whisky with Dambuie and adding decorative 'Langue de chat' biscuits in each serving.

ADRIAN'S BURNS NIGHT BANQUET

Menu and programme:

The Selkirk Grace
Cock-a-leekie soup
Piping in the Haggis
Haggis bashit neaps and champit tatties
Whisky toast and Address to a Haggis
Highland venison and winter vegetables served with fine wines
Toast to the lassies and Burns' poems
Atholl brose (Drambuie soaked raspberries, cream and oats)
Selection of Scottish cheeses served with oatcakes and bannocks
Choice of single malt, drambuie or port
Scottish dancing and modern tunes

ADRIAN'S COCK-A-LEEKIE SOUP

To serve 6-8

5 litres/8 pints water
1 small whole chicken or ½ a larger chicken
3 onions (chopped finely)
1.5 kg/4 lb leeks (chopped finely)
Salt
Freshly ground black pepper
Fresh herbs of your choice

Place the chicken into a large pan (the size of a pressure cooker) with the water and herbs and bring to the boil. Turn down the heat, cover and simmer for about one hour. The meat on the chicken should become soft. Strain the liquid off the chicken and put into a large bowl and leave to cool. Skim off any excess fat from the surface and reserve.

Take the chicken meat off from the bones and set aside. Melt the reserved fat in a large pan and cook the onions until softened. Add the leeks, cover and cook over a low heat for around five minutes, stirring occasionally. Add the strained stock and chicken meat to the pan and bring to the boil, then turn down the heat and simmer gently to heat through. Season, to taste, with salt and pepper and serve 'piping' hot.

ADRIAN'S BASHIT NEAPS AND CHAMPIT TATTIES

Bashit Neaps
500 g/1 lb turnips (swede), trimmed and peeled
2 tbsp butter
1 tsp grated ginger
Salt and freshly ground black pepper
Fresh chives for decoration (chopped)

Dice the swede and then boil in a large saucepan until tender. Drain in a colander and then return to the pan. Place over a very low heat for a few minutes, stirring, to remove the excess moisture. Add the butter and ginger to the pan and stir well. Cook for a few minutes, then mash until smooth. Season, to taste, with salt and pepper.

Champit Tatties
5 - 6 spring onions (finely chopped)
$1/2$ pint/300ml milk
2lb/1kg potatoes (Maris Piper are good), cooked, peeled and mashed
125 g/$4^{1}/_{2}$ oz butter
Salt
Freshly ground black pepper

The spring onions in this recipe can be replaced by fresh chives, fresh parsley, peas or even nettle tops. First chop the spring onions and place into a small pan with the milk and simmer gently for a few minutes until tender. Place the milk and greens into a pan with the mashed potato and butter. Season to taste with salt and freshly ground black pepper and place over a low heat. Cook the mixture, stirring well, for a few minutes, until smooth.

Using an ice cream scoop (or similar) place balls of the Bashit Neaps and Champit Tatties onto a baking tray and place either under a medium grill or oven until crisp on the outside. Then place servings of each onto plates and decorate with freshly chopped chives. The dish is now ready to receive the Haggis (after the famous Toast to the Haggis of course!).

Janet can always be relied on to make large batches of mince pies at Christmas and this is the recipe she has contributed.

JANET'S MINCE PIES

1 lb/450 g plain flour
½ lb/225 g butter
Luxury mincemeat

Rub the butter into the flour until crumb-like, adding a small amount of milk to bind together. Shape into 2-3 large balls and place in refrigerator for 1 hour.

Roll out pastry on a wooden pastry board and sprinkle a small amount of flour onto the board and rolling pin so the pastry does not stick. Roll out pastry until ¼ inch thick and cut out with a pastry cutter and use to line small pastry tins.

Add luxury mince meat about a generous tea spoon full per well. If lids are required, use a star-shaped cutter and add these to the bases pressing down lightly at the edges.

Cook at 180°C/350°F/Gas Mark 4 for 30 minutes checking regularly. When the pies are cooked, cool on a baking tray.

For iced mince pies, add white icing when cooled.

Stan and I invented this final dish in January 2003. He cooked the pork and the pasta while I made the sauce. It took less than 10 minutes to prepare.

ANNE AND STAN'S PORK AND PASTA

Serves 2

2 small pork steaks
Pasta for two
½ large onion
6 medium sliced mushrooms
1 stick celery, chopped
½ - 1 tsp dried basil
2 tbsp tomato purée
Tomato (chopped)
1 tbsp ketchup
1 tbsp olive Oil

Cook the pork steaks in a microwave oven (5 minutes), then cut them into strips. Cook the pasta separately.

Heat a non-stick pan and add olive oil, chopped onion and cook until softened. Add the sliced mushrooms and continue cooking, add chopped celery and tomato and stir well whilst cooking and add the dried basil.

Add the pork strips and mix. Add tomato purée and ketchup and stir well. Then add the soy sauce and mix well. Continue heating until all is hot. Drain the pasta and serve the sauce over it.

EPILOGUE

I FEEL that I have been extremely lucky to have had so many good friends and the many opportunities for travel abroad and meeting many interesting people from various countries. Travel is said to 'broaden the mind' and I have certainly found this to be true, especially when the travel is beyond the popular, often visited, holiday spots. Friendship with people from many different cultures has given me a much wider appreciation of how people approach things differently and, of course, how their needs are different. It also brings home how unequally the resources of the world are distributed. Most of this book is about people in affluent countries, who have plenty to eat and very good healthcare systems. But this is not true for much of the world, especially Africa.

So this brings me back to the main theme behind this book, which is to raise awareness of the need to provide better maternity services for people in poorer parts of the world. From the medical point of view, reducing maternal mortality is relatively easy to achieve. What is needed is a combination of medical expertise and facilities, the ability to deliver them where most needed and, of course, the funds to support the work. The Maternity Worldwide charity is providing the medical skills and infrastructure required, but they need financial help. You have already supported Maternity Worldwide in this important work through this book and many friends have already contributed through sponsoring various events, knitting baby vests and in a host of other ways. If you are not already a regular donor, please consider this and please let your friends know of Maternity Worldwide's work.

www.maternityworldwide.org

INDEX

Soup
Avocado soup	114
Broth	2
Butternut squash soup	115
Cock-a-leekie soup	116
Cold cucumber soup	30
Cream of mushroom soup	15
"Special" soup	64
Turkey and vegetable soup	92

Salad
Avocado, bacon and pine nut salad	20
Chopped green salad and dressing	1
Exotic chicken salad	71
Orange and almond salad	106
Vegetable trio jelloed salad	95

Meat
Australian meat pies	112
Babi ketchup	18
Barbecued spare ribs	5
Beef and vegetables, Chinese style	94
Beef goulash	70
Beef stroganoff	91
Cheddery cottage pie	33
Chicken and asparagus bake	16
Chicken and bacon tagliatelle	83
Chicken and mushroom lasagne	9
Chicken and okra curry	81
Chicken curry with chipatis	47
Chicken in red pesto sauce	19
Corned beef hot dish	38
Country chicken	93
Crisped chicory with ham and cheese	103
Crispy topped beef	29
Geordie curry	4
Lamb kovu	72
Meatloaf	49
Pork and pasta	119
Pork rib	101
Risotto a la Milanese	103
Risotto, low fat	99
Sweet and sour chicken	61
Swiss beef	75
Thai lamb curry	44
Tuscany chicken	98

Fish
Baked herring	51
Baked smoked haddock	59
Baked spiced fish	45
Baked stuffed salmon	52
Chilli-barbecued salmon with mango salsa	105
Cod bake	63
Cullen skink	42
Fish pie	48
Mackerel paté	17
Mixed fish paté	73
Mock crab sandwiches	74
Monkfish parcels	97
Omelette Arnold Bennett	58
Potted prawns	28
Salmon cutlets	80
Steamed fish, Chinese style	109

Vegetarian
Aromatic spiced chick peas	84
Bashit neaps	117
Champit tatties	117
Courgette flan with Hawaiian rice salad	31
Curried coleslaw	41
Jollof rice	113
Macaroni cheese	68
Mozzarella pesto and tomato on olive ciabatta	85

INDEX

Mushroom stroganoff	78
Penne with Quorn in a garlic and white wine sauce	82
Perfect pizzas	24
Shetland clapshott	56

Dessert

Apricot crunchie	35
Atholl brose (Aethelbrose)	79
Brown bread ice cream	13
Chocolate and lime mouse	35
Chocolate surprise pudding	22
Chocolate trifle	77
Crème brulée	7
Duke of Cambridge tart	76
Dulce de leche	104
Frozen apricot mousse	32
Jelly in a jiffy	110
Lemon cheesecake, easy-to-make	34
Lemon dainty	76
Lemon soufflé	39
Maracuja mousse (passion fruit)	30
Marmalade cream tart	41
Medieval pudding	27
Pear belle Helene	6
Pumpkin pie	88
Sticky toffee pudding	50
Summer pudding	14
Syllabub trifle	27
Tiramisu	8
Tiramisu, egg free	21

Cakes, pastries and biscuits

Banana sponge cake	23
Brown bread, quick	65
Brownies	90
Brussels cake	107
Cheese scones	57
Chocolate cake	10
Coconut surprise	46
Crème wafers	94
Crunchy coconut biscuits	26
Date and walnut loaf	36
Date balls	107
Fruit cake	26
Fruit scones	38
Gingerbread	40, 65
John Bull slab	57
Lemon crunch	73
Maids of honour	11
Maryland cookies	26
Mince pies	118
Oatcakes	63
Parkin	70
Peanut brownies	107
Praline cake	16
Scottish pancakes (drop scones)	64
Shetland bannocks	61
Shetland bronnie cake	56
Singing hinnies	11
Sponge cake	67
Toffee cake	12

Something different

'Best before' cheese spread	110
Damper	111
Kerasso (sour cherry liqueur)	100
Mint sauce	3
Sloe gin	17
Sticky bottoms	43
Walkers' revival	18